ATTENTION

Natural predators spend more time engaging life than they do taking it.

"In the final analysis, the business you have done and the deals you have closed have been a direct result of the doors you have opened."

-- Kivi Bernhard

PRAISE FOR THE BOOK.

"...an intriguing guide to business leadership and an exclusive approach that only someone with your background could deliver..."

Samuel A. Di Piazza, Jr., CEO - PricewaterhouseCoopers.

"..Having heard Kivi speak and having read his book, I remain impressed by the value and creativity he offers the business world. This book is a compelling read replete with rich information that is invaluable to executives, entrepreneurs, and individuals navigating today's sometimes complex and challenging business landscape.."

Ronald J. Savarese, SVP – Investments UBS

"... This book is unique in a refreshing way, and Bernhard's intellectual contrast between business success and the hunt of the African leopard was riveting! Read this book and you'll walk away with some new standards for your personal success strategy..."

Don Hutson, Co-author of the NY Times #1 Best-Seller, The One Minute Entrepreneur

"... I thought the book was very original. The use of the African wild kept the subject enjoyable and very different from all other business-related books that I own. My advice is to take it off the shelf and buy it..."

Fred Law, VP - Equifax Inc.

"…Kivi Bernhard's authenticity and experiential knowledge instantly spoke to my "leadership-mind". This book is beyond creative and informative, it captures the essence of Kivi's story and has the ability to redefine your "Hunt for Profit…"

John W. Wright II, Managing Partner - Northwestern Mutual

"…Your book is one that kept me most interested throughout its entirety. It is brilliant and insightful and will serve readers with great new knowledge…"

William F. Rubin, SVP – Swank Inc

LEOPARDOLOGY

The Hunt for Profit in a Tough Global Economy!

Kivi Bernhard

New York

LEOPARDOLOGY

The Hunt for Profit in a Tough Global Economy!

ISBN 978-1-60037-649-8 (pbk)
ISBN 978-1-60037-650-4 (hc)

Library of Congress Control Number: 2009904781

Cover Design by: Rachel Lopez
       Rachel@r2cdesign.com

MORGAN · JAMES
THE ENTREPRENEURIAL PUBLISHER

Morgan James Publishing, LLC
1225 Franklin Ave., STE 325
Garden City, NY 11530-1693
Toll Free 800-485-4943
www.MorganJamesPublishing.com

In an effort to support local communities, raise awareness and funds, Morgan James Publishing donates one percent of all book sales for the life of each book to Habitat for Humanity. Get involved today, visit **www.HelpHabitatForHumanity.org.**

Contents

Acknowledgements

The completion and publication of this book has been a lifetime goal and passion. I wish to take this opportunity to thank the Almighty for granting me life and affording me the opportunity to engage His world in health and in strength. I thank my parents, Rabbi Norman and Joan Bernhard, for teaching me how to see His world, and I thank my wife and best friend, Jordana, for teaching me what to do with what I see.

To my daughters, my four beautiful "diamonds," Suri, Bracha, Kaila and Goldie, you are why I persevere and push on in a world that assumes I will not succeed. Every single day, I fight "No" until it becomes "Yes" with the strength, encouragement and empowerment I receive from you and your mother. There is simply insufficient allowance on this page for me to adequately communicate the degree to which you children have taught me the value of connection and relationship. I am eternally indebted to each of you and have no words to thank you for the never-ending love and support that I receive from you.

Many have argued that trying to understand me, in general, is tough enough. Understanding what I write, however, takes an exceptional talent. That is just what I found in my outstanding editor, Dana Rubin, who was responsible not only for making sure the book retained my original voice, but also for translating it from "Kivi English" into English. Thank you, Dana, for going above and beyond.

Throughout my life, there have been many captains of industry, corporate CEO's, entrepreneurs and community leaders, who have afforded me time and access, allowing me to learn from their vast experience and knowledge. I thank them all for simply giving and expecting nothing in return.

Over the last few years, specifically, several giants of the professional speaking industry have unconditionally given of their time and expertise, simply because they believed in me. I truly and humbly thank them all, but, in particular, wish to mention the mentorship and guidance of the following great platform speakers and friends: Steve Rizzo, Nido Qubein, Jim Cathcart, Willey Jolly, Keith Harrell, Dan Thurman, Rob Waldo, Ken Futch, Gene Greissman, Phillip Van Hooser, Michele Arden-Stern, Steve Gardner, and Nancy Lauterbach.

Dedication

My business journey in the United States of America has been influenced by many associates and friends, all of whom have placed a unique brick in the construction of our enterprise.

However, I wish to dedicate this book to the indescribable friendship and business affiliation that I have been privileged to have with Ivan, Rayna, Howard and Anthony Solomon. It is simply difficult to articulate the trust, confidence and companionship that they have afforded me over the past eleven years. They are people of exceptional character and kindness and have truly served to exhibit to me and my family the capacity human beings have for refinement and honesty.

Introduction

"…and all the king's horses and all the king's men could not put **the world economy** back together again…" That's the bad news, folks; the good news is that you do not have to fix the world economy; you only have to fix your own. How? I have no idea. But, I can tell you where to begin: "Hunt Your Hunt!"

If you have picked up this book with the same expectations with which you have picked up so many other business, entrepreneurial, self-help, self-improvement or self-empowerment books, save your money and time, and put it back on the shelf. If you are expecting a clear, sure-fire, guaranteed list telling you "what to do to be successful" in these unprecedented economic times, (I know-- I have a shelf of them, too.), then you have the wrong book, and I cannot help you. I cannot give you a list of six things successful corporate leadership teams did to receive billions in "bailout" money, and how you can, too; or, nine things people who own successful laundromat chains do; or, 12 habits of highly lucky heirs to million dollar estates; or, 25 management tools for business owners which will guarantee that you become a publicly listed company in 24 hours; or, the seven things I did on the internet to become a millionaire, while fishing, and how you can do them, too, etc. No, unfortunately, dear reader, I do not have a crystal ball, and I do not know what our global economic future will be. I cannot guarantee you a pathway to success, or that you will achieve it when you arrive.

Here is the thing: Our world has dramatically changed in a matter of months. Market fundaments and truths, both financial and social, have literally been turned on their heads, forcing the collective consciousness to rethink what is real, and what is not; what is worth pursuing, and what is not; and, what is moral and ethical, and what is not. Every arena of our human world, as we know it, is being challenged to have truth triumph over confusion.

No, dear reader, I do not have a list of answers! And, if that is your expectation, I humbly apologize for disappointing you with this purchase. If it is too late, and you have already made a purchase of the book, please be comforted by the knowledge that you at least helped "stimulate" the US economy, as well as my own.

However, here is what I can do! I can humbly (ok, maybe not so humbly) share with you, in the most entertaining and articulate way possible, the incredible information, inspiration and motivation I received from Africa's most successful predator, when I was personally faced with just such an unknown and unpredictable time in my life. This, not only can I do, but it is, in fact, my honor and privilege to do so. It would be more than a lifetime accomplishment for me to know that there is, perhaps, even one nugget or anecdote of information that has spoken to you and shed light on your own "hunt" for success.

This book is not about me; it is about **you**. It is about the discovery of what you, as business owners, entrepreneurs or leaders already have, and not about what you, or the marketplace, think you may need. As you journey with me from tracking leopard deep in the African bush lands to initiating business in the high-rise boardrooms of corporations,

I do guarantee you one thing -- **me!** You will, at all times, get the unadulterated version of me, which my skillful editor, Dana Raymon Rubin, has worked so hard to maintain. Through **me**, I earnestly hope that **you** will discover **you**; because **you** are your market differentiator and the key to **your** success!

NatureNomics 101:

Natural predators actually spend more time engaging life than they do taking it! Counterintuitive, right? In fact, that is precisely the case. It is exactly their commitment to totally and fully engaging their "living" moments, which makes their "killing" moments so effective.

Man! I remember it as if it were a minute ago: that huge orbit of a sun, bursting colors of orange and yellow, exploding onto the African savannah! I was seven years old the first time my dad took me into the African bush; that crisp, early morning mist, grappling with those first rays of sunlight trying to make their way through; the dust, the sand and the grasslands all responding to the "Good Morning, Africa!" announcement that the sun had made as dawn broke.

I can smell it -- that distinct, early morning daybreak smell, indigenous to the African savannah that eerily asks you... "Who survived the night?" "Who was the hunter, and who was the hunted?" "Who ate, and who did not?" "Who 'closed the deal' and who did not?" I cannot tell you why or how, but I knew then, for all time, that Africa -- its rhythm and its wildlife-- would call to me my entire life. What I did not know was that it would be the majesty and precision of its most successful feline predator that would come to motivate and inform me during the course of some of my most challenging times. "Which one?" you ask. It is that beautiful and regal African leopard; a solo, solitary hunter; using stealth, cover and camouflage to establish itself as perhaps the most prolific, revered and successful predator on earth. I mean successful! I'm talking about a 76% close rate. Yep, it closes nearly three out of four of all "client prospects" it initiates; and, it does this alone, without the assistance of huge, corporate conglomerate help. Consider its competitors: lion, cheetah, hyena -- using the power of the pride and their strength in numbers -- but, "closing," on average, only 54% of their "client initiatives."

Sound familiar? You bet it does, because that is the current global marketplace in which you and I trade. Gone are the days of huge "lion pride" corporations with massive market share, human, infrastructural and financial resources. That belonged to yesteryear's economy.

Today, every dollar spent has a corporate accountant seeking its accountability, its efficiency and its efficacy -- Where did it go, and what did it do? So too, each individual is now scrutinized for accountability and productivity -- Where did he go, and what did he do?

Welcome to the human resource paradigm shift of our century. Successful teams are simply organized and empowered collections of successful individuals. Yes, the leopard uses the world around it as an asset for provision of cover and resource, but it instinctively depends on its own apparatus and tooling for results. It looks no further than the tip of its nose to know where the buck stops.

If it does not efficiently and effectively mobilize towards its "client opportunity," it simply will not eat. The corporation, organization or association is there to offer you a hunting ground, information, and, maybe, a parking space, if you are lucky. However, results and "client closure" lie with you.

This is what a corporate mission statement looks like in the African bush:

HUNT OR BE HUNTED.

Signed: G-d.

PS: Have a good day!

It's a funny thing; unlike most mission statements we often encounter, one really does not need a dictionary or thesaurus to understand this one. See, out there in the bush lands of Africa, there is a seemingly fundamental difficulty. There are no Arby's or McDonald's. You cannot get a sandwich at Subway or "order in" Domino's. There are no Starbucks. "Customers" are not ready-made and packaged; they exist only in concept and must be evaluated, and reevaluated, from initial prospect to client closure.

In truth, with all our executive education and finessed terminology of micro and macro economics, etc., this primordial and age-old truth really remains the maxim of both successful teams as well as successful individuals. The ability to remain "result-centric" rather than "process-centric" and to move away from an "It will happen..." to an "I will make it happen..." attitude is what will determine the "hunter" from the "hunted" in the post "bail-out" economy we live in today.

The African leopard is held in high regard by great African cultures such as the Zulu people. It is known as the "master hunter," and the African leopard has come to serve as a symbol of courage, strength, perseverance and perfection -- the way G-d intended it. Perhaps, because of my upbringing as an Orthodox Jew, or because of the specific parents I was gifted, the notion that we are made and built for success was something I always took literally. In my youth, it never occurred to me otherwise. It was only after I entered the working world as a young, married man in Johannesburg, South Africa that I began to understand that there are really people out there who think this is not so. This was shocking new information for me. I mean, the idea that I need to read something, hear something, wear something or be something in order to be successful was, quite frankly, as foreign a notion to me as the prospect of becoming the next Pope.

The idea that the default position for man is inherent deficiency, and that he can only succeed if he imports proficiency from the outside, was absurd to me. I grew up being taught that G-d does not make junk! I believed it and owned it, and, I am here to share with you that I still do.

It's that simple. You have what you need to succeed. What you do not have, you do not need.

Oh, brother -- was I challenged to believe my own beliefs! It was 1997 when my family experienced some real turbulence upon our decision to relocate to the United States of America from my birthplace of Johannesburg, South Africa. My wife and I, and our four beautiful daughters and thirteen pieces of luggage, arrived at the newly built Pittsburgh International Airport on a Tuesday morning in August. It took only the drive to my parents-in-law's home to realize that the airport was the one and only thing in Pittsburgh that was newly built. But hey, it was now home, and, together with prayer, energy and the check in my pocket for $860.22, this was our new reality. I was a foreigner in a foreign country, culture and, yes, language. Many people still argue that I don't speak English!

Welcome to America!

Chapter 1

Leopardology ™

The Birth of
"Positive Predatory Thinking" ™

RELAX! NO, WE'RE not "preying" on our clients and "killing" our customers with predatory schemes in the tradition of the Enrons and Bernie Madoffs of the world. We are, however, looking to adopt the focused, result-centric and purposeful living habits in which Africa's most successful predators instinctively engage -- day in and day out. And, somehow they manage to do so without Facebook or LinkedIn.

Here's the deal. On our drive home from the airport, I noticed a sign. (Leopard do this; they continually take inventory of the market environment and record it for later use.) The sign, posted by the United Methodist Church of Pittsburgh, read "Donate Your Car or Boat." Well, the day after we settled into my parents-in-law's basement, off I went to the church (although, not before I went to the Mellon Bank to establish an account and make a deposit for $860.22). Now, like a good Jewish boy, I knocked on the door of the United Methodist Church. At first, Father McCormick was disconcerted at opening the doors of the church to an Orthodox Jew, but soon said, "Please come in, and how may I help you, son?" – his eyes still fixed on my yarmulke. My question was not actually of a religious or spiritual nature. I simply wanted to know if, perhaps, the church had any of those donated cars for sale. I was in luck! Father McCormick took me out back and showed me a white, 1987 Mazda 626 manual shift with only 112, 000 miles on the clock. This was good! (In South Africa, most cars are manual shift.) "How much is the car?" I asked. "Well, my son," said the pastor, "the church is asking $400.00 for the car."

I instantly saw my working capital diminish by half. I have mentioned that I am Jewish, and, therefore, you clearly understand that there is simply no way I can pay retail for anything I buy! So, in my kindest voice possible, I asked Father McCormick if he would take $200.00 for the car. After hearing a well-delivered sermon on the virtues of charity and community needs, I finally made my last offer at $250.00, which was accepted by the church. Thus, my friends, my first transaction in the United States was made, and my business career had begun.

Earlier in the morning, while at the Mellon Bank, I had seen the large K-Mart sign across the road advertising an in-store "business card printing machine." It was great! You could give the machine ten bucks, and it would give you 100 business cards. My card was simple. It read: "Kivi Bernhard, International Diamond Wholesaler," and offered my father-in-law's home telephone number at the bottom of the card. That afternoon, armed with the "jewelers" listings of a Yellow Pages of Greater Pittsburgh, 100 business cards, and a 1987 Mazda 626 that needed a clutch, I was in business. Through a contact of my father's, I had arranged a line of credit for $10,000.00 with a South African cutter that had an office in New York with a toll-free number.

One small difficulty became evident. The diamond and jewelry industry apparently had existed in the United States well before my arrival. Shockingly, it turns out, vendors had been supplying retail jewelers with service and inventory for almost 100 years. This detail constantly got in my way and prevented me from doing business. Oh, and one other thing I got a lot... "Who the heck are you, Buddy?" The loose diamond business is about trust, integrity, honesty, performance history and a time-tested business relationship between the parties. You clearly understand why these components were a problem for me! I began to give new meaning to the word "rejection" and simply could not get to the right people at the right time with the right history.

All I heard was "No." Now, my wife has always told me that I don't hear a thing she or anyone else says. She must be right, because I just kept pushing forward, literally ignoring my lack of results. When I was a kid, my father would always say that "perseverance has succeeded where genius has failed," and, so, with total commitment and energy, I continued to knock on doors, unaware that there was a critical dimension missing in my market approach.

From The Bush To The Boardroom!

Pittsburgh --It was gray; it was cold; it was old. It was far from my home, and it was far from my other "love," sunny South Africa and its glorious natural beauty and wildlife. It was difficult --very difficult!

Who would have imagined that it would be those deeply embedded memories of Africa and its predators that would come to motivate me through this extraordinarily difficult time? The critical strategy, focus, leadership initiative and change management methodology of that magnificent African leopard would come to be the thing that kept me on the hunt for clients and customers. So was born Leopardology™ and the extreme privilege and blessing I have to share it with others the world over.

The Six Pillars of Positive Predatory Thinking ™

You got it! -- Six pillars of critical business thinking and strategy gleaned from the hunting habits and techniques of the African leopard. Hey, this stuff has been incorporated into MBA, EMBA and professional selling programs of leading business schools and universities! As I drove those highways and byways of Pennsylvania, West Virginia and Ohio, looking for retail jewelers in a foreign country, an amazing thing began to happen. With the visual impact and detail of a large HD TV screen, my mind began to play back those incredible scenes of lion, hyena, cheetah and leopard on the hunt in their "**marketplace**," moving with such dedication towards their "**client**." In great detail and slow motion, I would recall their every step, pre and post hunt, analyzing their exact strategy and precision. What a privilege it had been all those years to see G-d's perfection in motion, as demonstrated by these finessed "deal closers."

But it was that leopard, "ingwe" in Zulu, a solo, solitary hunter, void of outside resources to get its "business" done, which came to propel me through what seemed like an impossible and insurmountable task. That leopard was me, alone and isolated in a huge marketplace that needed another diamond dealer like a desert needs sand! The leopard's daily requirement to self initiate and mobilize so spoke to me, because that was exactly my scenario. I was required to be the entire operation: spot the deal, hunt the deal, close the deal and retain the deal, all alone -- that was me. I know you are reading this thinking, "That is ME!"

So were born the "Six Pillars of **Positive** Predatory Thinking" ™.

Giraffe Envy!

It must have been about 5:30 am on a Tuesday morning, and we were deep in the bush lands of Polekwane, South Africa, engulfed in G-d's world. Groggy-eyed but pumped to be in the African bush, I awoke to see Lukas, my friend and Zulu tracker, preparing his morning tea on a twig fire he had made. It was another glorious day in Africa, and the cool crisp air was already telling us of the excitement and tension of the unknown that lay ahead.

As we gave each other the traditional Zulu greeting of "sawubona," I joined Lukas, sitting on the remains of a log we had burned the night before. We then sat for a while, having a robust and comprehensive conversation in total silence – in Africa you can do this!

Taking in the sights and sounds of the bird life around us and the hippos calling from the Nwetzi River, we were both having a serious "bush talk."

What amazing gift of nature will we experience today? What phenomena of the animal kingdom will I learn of today? What will we see? What will we not see? And of course, the big question whenever I am in the bush: Will I see my "ingwe" (leopard) today?

Every move Lukas makes has intent, has purpose and has meaning. He is only 58 years old but carries with him bush wisdom, life stories and truths that span a lineage of several generations. In short, Lukas is a highly intelligent, though illiterate, African bush version of Socrates. There is a life lesson around every corner and at the end of every conversation. Without introduction, Lukas turned to me, and, in a soft voice, said, "It is now five generations my family has lived in the bush. We have never heard of a leopard that wants to be a giraffe!" Lukas looked at me for a short while, waiting for my eyes to let him know that I had just caught what he had said, then smiled and turned back to stir his tea which was now hot. After I had processed his statement --I mean the full extent of its depth -- I smiled, and then chuckled --at myself!

What the heck is the deal with us humans? What is this need we have to continually seek to be something we are not? What is the source of this disease that has so afflicted society? It is insane. It is perhaps the single largest contributor to people's inefficiency and their inability to achieve their goals. The cardiologist wants to be a pilot; the pilot wants to be a professional golfer; the golfer wants to be the UPS guy, who wants to be a CEO. By the way, the CEO wants to be a cardiologist.

This touches on something I often speak about; I call it "pre-sentism." Just as it sounds, it is the ability to be absolutely present and engaged in your very own life. Allow me to repeat that – **"your life!"** Imagine viscerally believing that you are built for success and have what you need to succeed; imagine spending time with yourself, just as you are, in your perfection, without the desire or need to be something else or someone else -- and, enjoying it! Human behavior dictates that, if you can destroy a man's sense of self, then you can destroy his ability to be effective. If you can shake someone at the core, in his essence, in terms of who and what he is, he will self-destruct from the inside out.

But, here is the magic, ladies and gentleman: The opposite is equally so; if you cannot disturb a man's relationship with self, if you cannot separate him from his innate belief that he is "good to go," then you cannot disturb his ability to succeed. If one's core as a human being is sacred and untouchable, then he is unshakable and cannot be prevented from achieving -- even from the outside in. The animal world does this instinctively; we, as humans, have to choose to do so. I ask you, have you ever heard of a leopard that wants to be a giraffe?

Lukas had taught me a fundamental and critical truth of life and leadership. What he did not know was that this idea would become the cornerstone of a business keynote that would be shared with tens of thousands of sales, leadership and business teams all over the world. This concept would form the very premise of Leopardology™ and the art of Positive Predatory Thinking ™.

Welcome to Leopardology ™.

Chapter 2

Why Leopard Never Take Prozac!

Positive Predatory Pillar ™ No.1

In the bush.

Know what you are: The leopard has a clear and undisturbed relationship with all of its tooling and apparatus, allowing it to deploy and use its entire being while on the hunt.

Take all of you to the market and to your workplace -- you are your market differentiator!

AS I LOOKED into the long spear grass, I could vaguely make out her head. I took a peek through my binoculars, and her silhouette became clear to me. Even with my well-trained "bush eyes," her camouflage was just so precise; it was tough, in fact, to make out where the bush ended and she began.

My buddy, Howard, who was driving our 4x4, saw her way before I did and had a fixed position on exactly where she was lying. It was a late afternoon sun, and the golden yellow rays were working in perfect synthesis with the golden yellow flickers coming off the grass. Howard kept on pointing and positioning my binoculars, but it was not until I suddenly saw her large tongue whip across her face as she began grooming herself, that I finally had a clear fix on her. What a magnificent and beautiful female leopard she was! We spent the next 15 or so minutes watching this perfect specimen in her natural habitat. What a privilege that was!

The common wisdom suggests that predators, using their tongues, continually groom themselves as part of a combined health and well-being program -- courtesy of nature. They apply large amounts of saliva onto their coats and other exposed areas mixed with valuable Vitamin K found in natural sunlight. Aside from helping to protect them against harmful ticks and parasites, this practice also helps regulate their body temperature in the hot African sun.

Leopard are groomers extraordinaire and will spend a disproportionate amount of time meticulously grooming themselves in a way that lion, cheetah and other large cats do not. It seems that with leopard, there is something much larger taking place throughout this entire grooming process. There is! They are taking inventory and re-acquainting themselves with themselves. They are literally revisiting their exact equipment and tooling, studying it and banking it to memory. As they pass that powerful serrated tongue through their coat, they will actually take a mental note of their current body condition, toning and viability.

Everything gets a "licking": old injuries, new injuries, wounds that have healed and those that have not; paws, claws, teeth, ears, eyes, nose and toes -- a total quality control and "market" readiness assessment. As they move through the grooming ritual, they will roll over, stand up, lie down and stand back up again, moving towards a tree trunk for some back scratching and tick removing. All of this allows for a complete performance evaluation and inventory "take" as to exactly what assets it can fully depend on while on the next hunt. It is an ingenious methodology that allows the leopard to not only assess performance, but to reinforce and, once again, ingrain this acute sense of self and trust that leopard have for their very own tooling and apparatus.

So, why then would a leopard take Prozac? Now, I am with you, and I know that you know that I know that there is real medicinal benefit and value to Prozac. In fact, it might help people become clearer about who they are, but I am referencing it as we know it colloquially – you know, a "shrink" drug. (Work with me here, people.) Meaning: If you had a total and unequivocal relationship with your entire being, believing it to be indispensable to your very success, why would you want to change your perception of your **you**? You see, leopard have an undisturbed relationship with their tooling apparatus and original "factory issue" equipment. They instinctively know that their G-d-given equipment is truly their key for survival. They are acutely aware, intrinsically, that they have been built for success, because G-d does not make junk. Furthermore, they have not watched enough television to come to believe that society and the world around them are rooting for their failure. They assume success as an instinctive, natural default position and have not had the pleasure of spending time on someone's couch, being told that, due to childhood and parental mismanagement, success is not an option. When you have this kind and degree of relationship with yourself, the very last thing you would want to do would be to change and alter your perception of who and what you are. Your very hunt for survival depends on **you** -- why would you want to alter that?

"Look Mom, three inch canines and no hands..."

Let's take a look at some of this equipment and tooling that leopard so inherently trust.

The "Big Guy" upstairs put some serious stuff on the leopard conveyor belt assembly line. I mean there is some heavy-duty equipment on this finessed hunter and "deal closer." Leopard have incredible musculature and upper body strength. They are able to lift prey, sometimes twice their own body weight, 15 to 20 feet up in a tree, where they will feed on their "client." Their upper torso houses massive musculature that extends all the way through their neck and into their jaw line. Leopard have an uncanny ability to hear even the slightest sounds some 500 feet off in the distance. Having extraordinary vision, they require only one sixth of the light we humans require for perfect vision. Because leopard are tree climbers, they have particularly well-developed claws, especially their infamous drew claw, which has been known to reach two inches in size. Around campfires, under African skies, many stories and tales have been told by hunters and villagers about that renowned leopard claw that never fully retracts -- its strength, its power and the damage it can and has caused. With the assistance of extremely well-developed jaw muscles, leopard present lower and upper canine teeth that can measure three inches in a fully developed male. They have been known to bite through solid bone, two inches thick. Beyond their ability to penetrate and bite through flesh, these teeth offer the leopard a unique opportunity to "close" their prey in total and absolute silence. By ensuring that these canine teeth have sealed off the airway and windpipe of their prey, leopard prevent any distress call that may alert other predators. This ingenious closing technique helps leopard prevent losing existing "clients" to competitors. Added to this ability they have to harness the power of stealth and silence is the ability to maneuver and manipulate their entire bodies for maximum cover while on the hunt.

With extraordinary agility, leopard will contour their bodies to the environment around them, thereby obtaining maximum cover and allowing them to remain undetected by potential prey. Their entire modus operandi is about stealth and cover, and, as such, they will exert tremendous energy, effort and patience in setting up a hunt. They naturally come by the stamina that is needed for such a hunting methodology, and this explains why their "close rate" is so incredibly high. Leopard can move vast distances with little water, and, compared with their competitors, require far less "down time" to recover from the exhaustion of the hunt. Their sense of smell is fabulously well-developed, but, cleverly, rather than using it to detect scavenging opportunities like hyena do, leopard use the sense of smell to quickly establish the presence of competitor predators. They use this with amazing accuracy to reestablish the risk and potential return-on-investment of the hunt at hand -- and to act accordingly. Their willingness to step back from a hunt is as amazing as their ability to step into it.

Leopard are, perhaps, best known for their exquisite coat, which is renowned not only for its beauty, but for the extraordinary camouflage that it offers its wearer. Clearly the epitome of the mastery of G-d's paintwork, leopard's coats allow them to remain almost undetected in the African bush. You literally cannot see them! This is part and parcel of what makes them so dangerous to encounter in their natural habitat. It is very difficult to see them from afar, and when you encounter them close up, well, you are way too close for the story to end well! It is with such precision that their coats blend with the terrain around them, that, in fact, leopard from different regions can be identified from the exact reddish/brownish hue in their coat, matching perfectly the color range in their home soil. The camouflage of the leopard is truly renowned in the animal kingdom and is the stuff of much folklore and riveting stories of game hunters who never returned.

But without doubt, the undisputed "magnus opus" of the African leopard is its astonishing ability to tree its prey. You've got it, baby! As mentioned earlier, leopard will take prey that might be three times their own body weight and hoist it twenty feet up into a tree, which will serve as a holding environment ("client retention" - more about this later). This unexplained zoological phenomenon is not only an awesome sight to behold, it is also an unparalleled display of sheer power and strength not to be duplicated on earth.

Now, that's what I'm talking about! And, heck yeah – if that's what G-d gave me, I'm **trusting** it all the way to the "bank!"

Find it. Kill it. Eat it... I'm here to hunt!

We were in a bush camp in South Africa by the name of Shimuweni. This beautiful, small camp is nestled in a remote section of the middle region of the great Kruger National Park. It was March, and the weather was glorious. It was at the end of a long day that started well before 5:00 am. I was sitting in a thatch hide that overlooked the Letaba River with a sundowner in one hand and a pair of binoculars in the other. By now you know, I was in heaven. It was gorgeous -- I mean seriously gorgeous; the sun was just setting behind the "koppies" (hilltops) in the distance, and the yellow light, with its deep orange overture, offered sufficient visibility to still see much of the activity on the river. The usual suspects were present; hippos in the water, crocodile just beginning to move off the sand banks and slip into the water, a pair of saddle billed storks, an African spoonbill in the reeds, some crowned lapwings, and a small herd of some 15 impala, knowing to stand well back from the water's edge. I was not on dinner duty that night, and I was alone in the hide, watching the "nature channel" in a big way!

I had made a complete scan, east to west, of the entire panoramic view in front of me, (in fact several times), and was just about to kick back and relax, when my unaided eye caught the flickering of its right ear. "No way!" I said, literally gasping for breath -- "No (bleep) way!" I repeated, enunciating each letter to demonstrate my disbelief as to what my brain was telling me I might see unfold before me. There it was, across the river on the northwest bank. This was a huge and experienced territorial male. As if he could hear me breathing, his rotating ears fixed in my direction and locked in for a moment of analysis before he turned his entire head my way. I leaned forward to acknowledge his gesture to me, knocking over my glass of Chivas Regal on the rocks, as I set my eyes into my binoculars. This was one of the most spectacular leopard sightings I have ever had. It was not just the beauty of this specific specimen, or the fact that it was hunting, but it was the glorious setting of the African sun, kissing the waters of the Letaba River, that made this so idyllic and majestic.

My heart told me to run and call my friend Howard (yeah, the same Howard as previously mentioned, a good friend and another "bush junky" with whom I have spent a lot of time in the African bush, and whose name you will see referenced often) to get to the hide "STAT!" My brain, however, told me that it would cost me a once in a lifetime wildlife viewing opportunity – a potential leopard hunt from beginning to end. Besides, it truly would have required plastic surgery or a pneumatic jackhammer to get those binoculars out of my hands! So, I did both. Silently moving back, while fixed on what was taking place some 500 feet ahead of me, I found my way to the entrance of the hide and called my buddy in a quiet whisper. Although light was beginning to fade, we were still able to clearly see all the players involved. There were several choice, potential picks in the herd of impala, which were now separated from the leopard by maybe 200 feet of river brush, rocks, sandbars and pockets of African pussy willows. He was upwind and had a perfect "20" (visual) on their every movement.

The impala, having not the slightest clue that one of them was about to engage in a long term "client relationship" with a leopard, could not see him, hear him or smell him. Instinctively knowing this to be a dangerous time of day, they nervously continued to graze, spending most of their time keeping watch.

As that golden orb of a sun continued to drop below the horizon, our visual on the leopard began to fade. We could still clearly see his head and upper torso, but the rest of him simply faded into the rock and river brush alongside him, precisely as his incredible camouflage intended. We knew we were fighting the clock, and that we had maybe 8 to 12 minutes of viable daylight left.

We were both exhilarated and edgy that nature's clock was not in sync with ours. Both of us were just locked on the incredible scene that was taking place ahead of us. You could hear Howard and me in a whispered banter of all sorts of "couch commentaries," some of which were not PG 13, but all of which reflected the magnificence of surrendering to G-d's great world. After a short silence that somehow came over us, Howard broke out with the following, in a mix of cultural and colloquial South African English, Afrikaans and Yiddish and said the following:

....nu! china...is this boytchick going to make a move here, or are we going to get b'donned by this b'kakta shvitzidikke sun...brother, please... show some enthusiasm here and do your thing, boetie china...are you waiting for Pretoria to send you an invitation to hunt?

Now for my fellow South Africans reading this, I know you are "laaging" yourself sick right now! But for my other readers please allow me to loosely translate Howard's little expletive as follows:

Mr. Leopard, are you going to do something here and hunt that impala in front of you, or are we going to miss seeing this truly once in a lifetime leopard hunt because of the failing sunlight? You need to eat; there is food; it's in reach and doable -- what's your hesitation?

After I regained control of my lung function from laughing so hard and so quietly, I looked at Howard and said, "Howie, this is a leopard; the hunt is over -- just not yet."

Folks, the news is not good -- for us and the impala that is! I know you are all edgy to know how this ended, and if we saw it. It ended alright, but no, we did not see it. It was perhaps 15 minutes later when we heard it all go down, but well under the cover of a set sun. It was a brief, swift and decisive commotion that happened seconds after we heard the alarm call ring out from the alpha male impala that did its best to warn its harem. It was also some 100 feet further back in the bush from where they had been -- a better site location for the leopard – no crocodile at the water's edge to contend with.

Now here is the lesson and a critical element of Positive Predatory Pillar No.1 – Know What **You** Are.

Yes, Howard and I were enormously frustrated and disappointed not to see the hunt play out. I have been going into the African bush for 34 years and have had the privilege to see a complete hunt on only two occasions. It is extremely rare and tough to be in the right place at the right time. However, I wish to make a larger point.

The hunt happened! That's the point. The hunt, in fact, happened before it happened, and that is what I was communicating to Howard. Here is what I mean: When leopard get out into the "market place," they are there to do business and "close deals." Well before the hunt, they are totally convicted about their objective and have an **absolute** and **unapologetic** relationship with the result-centric approach they take. They have taken total -- and here is the key word -- "ownership" of the result and objective long before they move out on the hunt. "The hunt is over," "the deal is done," before it starts – so to speak. All they need to do now is back into the logistics of how and when.

The notion that they are going to find a food source, kill it and eat it, is **not** the variable and **not** up for negotiation.

They own the result before it is ever achieved. The reason they own the result is that they own the requirement that generated the result -- the need to eat! They are unconflicted, unequivocal and uncomplicated regarding their ability to get food!

There is a beauty and fundamental learning opportunity in this lesson from the wild. We humans continually sabotage our business and life efforts by complicating, confusing and convoluting our basic "ownership" of our own right and ability to be successful. We human beings are truly masters of confusion.

Instinctive as it may be, it is this comprehensive belief in self, and a total commitment to this self, that allows this majestic predator leopard to simply know what it is and take all of itself into the "market." While it might not be that "digestible" to us humans, it is truly this simple in its raw form:

"I am a leopard. I have been given everything I need to succeed and eat in life. I will not apologize for my hunting ability and have only one question I am willing to entertain: Is it dead yet, and can I eat it?"

(Taken from the Leopard 12-Step Program Manual.)

Chapter 3

The "GET-IT" Crisis of 2008!

Positive Predatory Pillar ™ No.1

In the boardroom.

Know what you are: The leopard has a clear and undisturbed relationship with all of its tooling and apparatus, allowing it to deploy and use its entire being while on the hunt.

Take all of you to the market and to your workplace -- you are your market differentiator!

IT HAS BEEN called the "Credit Crisis of 2008." I would like to suggest that it had nothing to do with either "credit" or "crisis." While it may have culminated in 2008, clearly it was an accumulation of misuse and abuse over the past twenty years. By the same token, while it may have culminated and manifested in a credit crisis, it was generated by a global, en masse willingness on the part of society to perceive value where, in fact, it did not exist --hence, the credit crisis.

However, upon closer examination of this crisis, anyone, with even one honest eye still open, has to conclude that it was not just with money that we perceived and believed inflated value. Not at all, and, in fact, money was at the end of the chain. Here is what I am sharing. Our culture has been extraordinarily successful over the last twenty years in packaging and delivering offerings of inflated value across every spectrum of human consumption. We have elevated successful actors and celebrities to the position of social and political commentators. We have elevated successful sportsmen and sportswomen to the position of social role models. We have taken brand-name perfumes, clothing and cigarettes and elevated them to the point that they are perceived to be indispensable to achieving success. We have taken politicians, statesmen, international organizations and lobbyists and given them free rent in the minds and souls of our student population, elevating their opinions to the veracity of the Bible itself. We have elevated the speculation, opinions and sophisticated offerings of industry leaders and financial captains to unreasonable heights, where they remain unchallenged and unverified. We have allowed the sleek and slick use of technology and digital high-definition broadcasting to give unprecedented value and integrity to the opinions and speculation offered in the media. We have elevated and inflated the value of a document, broadcast, video or e-mail exchange, simply because it came to us via cyberspace or a blog. Ultimately, this has become a way of life and a thinking pattern that is perfectly acceptable, and, in fact, lauded by society.

So, when Fannie Mae programs, along with the entire financial instrumentation that supports the mortgage and real estate industry, chooses to do the same -- inflate the value -- why are we surprised?

What's the shock? If I have an inflated perception about everything else around me, why would this not include the realm of brick and mortar? Hence, I submit to you that what we have really experienced is a "Get-It" crisis. That's correct -- a mass refusal on the part of the international community of human beings to actually "get it!" Get what? -- Get that the ultimate expression of humanity, which distinguishes us from the animal world, is the ability to delineate, to decide, to identify and to articulate between that which is "real" and that which is not – meaning, that which has "value" and that which does not. (I know, I have read Nietzsche, and it is not my intention to plunge into the philosophical question of whether or not anything is, in fact, "real.") This ability we have as human beings to decipher and choose, rather than digest and consume, has been, and will continue to be, the differentiator between us and the animal world.

So, when we choose as individuals to ignore and dismiss our freedom and ability to choose, we not only cheat ourselves out of the ultimate human experience, we also penalize ourselves in the marketplace. We handicap ourselves! By insisting on living as an "unconscious consumer" rather than a "chooser," we permanently spend our lives importing resources from the outside. We look around us and ferociously explore what options are available to us from the outside that we can consume in an effort to achieve success. We don't "get it!" We don't get that we are human beings with specific, particular and indispensable tooling that has been individually designed for our personal success. The game of life is for us to "get it," not "cred-it." Perceive and buy the value on hand here and now, not that which is on tap in the future! Choose to embrace the notion that we are built for success! And, that, with surgical precision, we have been given exactly what it is that each of us needs to achieve the individual success that is intended for us. The opportunity is for us to become exporters of our own individual selves rather than importers of everyone else's. We don't do this, do we? We go out there into the marketplace and seek to conform to the standard "sameness" that is currently in vogue. And, if we don't have it, we will go and buy it -- whatever it may be!

So often, I recall that majestic African leopard and its steadfast, unequivocal and unrelenting commitment to itself, to its own tooling, and to its own equipment -- a passionate commitment to using what it does have, refusing to dwell on what it does not have -- living in the realm of "**have**," not "**need**." So often, I am envious that it does so instinctively, while I have to choose to do so.

Leadership, Not "Findership!"

It is 1997. Here I am in the USA, trying to sell loose diamonds to retail jewelers and diamond dealers. I throw everything I have at them just to open doors -- price, product, delivery, terms, etc.

Those doors were just slamming. I simply was not gaining entry into their buying psyche; there was a button I just was not pushing, and it was frustrating me no end. I had huge responsibility – like a family, depending on me for food, shelter, clothing and one or two other small details like medical insurance and schooling…small stuff! I had been in the country a month or two, and it was quickly becoming clear to me that I was in a foreign culture, with a foreign climate, topography and even language. I truly thought that I was not only competitive, but very much competing, and could simply not understand why I wasn't gaining client entry. I was spending large amounts of time analyzing inventory, service provision, market conditions, consumer demand, pricing and marketing. It all looked good! I mean really good! What's the problem here, people? I have loose diamonds to sell.

You, Mr. & Mrs. Retail Jeweler, have customers looking to buy loose diamonds and need a vendor to supply you diamonds. I am honest; I am trustworthy; I have good product and good pricing, and my offering is competitive – and hey, I'm a nice guy! What the heck is the problem? Why are we not doing business?

It was at the end of 1999, two years after having set up my wholesale loose diamond business, when I found myself attempting to develop and bring on board a prospective client located in Cincinnati, Ohio. This was a substantial, free standing, independent retail jeweler, who certainly had not been waiting for me to arrive from Johannesburg, South Africa. Three generations old, with vendor relationships that were twice my age, this business clearly had no apparent "need" that was waiting for me to address. Initially, I simply walked in the door in an unabashed and ruthless attempt to compete with my competitor vendors. Whatever my competition can do, so can I... whatever they provide you, however they service you, how well they price you, so can I. The door was simply slamming, and I was unable to even get in front of the diamond buyer.

It was on the cold, dark drive back to Pittsburgh, Pennsylvania, where we were living at the time, that the "penny dropped" and "Positive Predatory Pillar No. 1" hit me. The built-in movie theatre in my head started to play back scenes of the African savannah and its predators, of which I had such fondness -- that majestic leopard that I had been privileged to see so many times, deep in the African bush land; its non-negotiable insistence on grooming itself and continually taking inventory of its personal resources and apparatus; that unique and evident "knowledge-of-self" that it communicates with those penetrating eyes; an unexcused awareness that it is perhaps the most successful and dangerous feline predator on earth -- no apologies offered.

"Of course!" I blurted out to myself, as the fundamental mistake I was making became crystal clear. As I unpacked my thoughts, I realized that I was not giving my prospective client anything which this client did not already have, and it had not occurred to me to give this client the one thing that only **I** can.

In that moment, I acutely understood that what I can bring to my prospect's business, that my competitors cannot, is **me,** the element of which I had taken the least inventory and upon which I had placed the least significance.

My single biggest advantage, asset, and "value-add" had been left in the car outside and had not at all been offered to my prospective client. Immediately, I acknowledged that I needed to do what I had seen the leopard instinctively do.

I had to embark on a deep, introspective study of who and what I am with implacable, intellectual honesty. I had to get hold of exactly what my specific tooling is and what my particular apparatus includes, bank it to memory and become inseparable from this knowledge. This would allow me to clearly know what defines **me** from the person next to me, to package this information and to take it with me "on **my** hunt" to the marketplace.

Two months later, with a completely revamped business card, dress code and aura that accurately reflected me, I went back to Cincinnati. As part of a "positive predatory" strategy, I chose not to make an appointment with the buyer and walked into the store unexpectedly. Fortuitously, the buyer was in. I asked the receptionist to please tell the buyer that I was in the store, and that I had absolutely no merchandise with me at all.

After ten minutes or so, the buyer came down with that "Oh, bleep…it's a diamond salesman" look on her face. Quickly she learned that I really had no diamonds to sell her. She was now confused and amused and said, "You traveled here without a single diamond to show me?" In my thickest South African accent, I responded as follows: "I made a 600 mile round trip to share with you that diamonds are what we transact, but it is a business relationship with me, Kivi Bernhard, that I sell." Having now gained her visceral attention, I went on to articulate to her "who and what" I am, touching on core fundamentals of what makes me **me**. I was able to communicate that my contribution to their corporation would far exceed product, price and service.

Rather, it would be **me** that they would be buying and the things I aspire to stand for, namely: honesty, integrity, faith based practices, family values, and, yes, gemological expertise. We soon began doing business together and continue to grow from strength to strength to this day.

It was this encounter that helped me create our most successful business slogan: "A diamond is easily obtained -- An honest dealer, however, is indeed a rare gem."™ . I had made the most primordial mistake man can make. I had entirely discounted and ignored the truly irreplaceable component of my market offering -- **me!**

Particularly in this current global economy, which is still reeling from the effects of the credit crisis and liquidity freeze, any attempt to penetrate the consumer market needs to have its market differentiator lead the charge. Through their misguided behavior, major captains of industry and leading financial executives have stripped the consumer of the fundamentals of trust and integrity. Consumer confidence in the "good will" of man and "intent for mutual prosperity" has been severely damaged. The corporations, organizations, associations and clients that you're looking to sell, lead or engage on any level, need to be able to instantaneously perceive and "get" a sense of comfort before they are willing to even consider transacting with you.

Ok, deep breaths and another swig of coffee. Folks, follow me here for a moment: The only opportunity an individual or a corporate entity has to instantly communicate this component of market differentiation to a potential client lies in its ability to efficiently and effectively mobilize this very **you** factor -- to immediately be able to transfer a differentiator which indicates that their entire being, personality and very essence as a human being is present and will, in fact, be the dominant offering during the course of any potential transaction.

In the business world, we use the word "*leader*" like we use the word "*manager*." It simply describes a level of responsibility and experience within the structure of an organization. Well, this could not be further from what truly distinguishes leaders from the rest of the pack. And no, it's not that "leaders" read four books a day before 6:30 am, and that they write down 23 new ideas before noon, etc. All consistent deal closers and business leaders know that their differentiating factor is their ability to deal in the realm of "have." Correct – they live in a place and space of what is at their disposal, as opposed to what is not. They study and take inventory of their "hunting apparatus and territory," their tooling and their equipment -- committing to it as it is and taking it into the marketplace. This is a leader -- someone who leads himself and others to what already exists, not to that which does not.

As I have traveled and observed the inner workings of corporations and organizations the world over, it has been confirmed for me that there truly are simply two default positions: there are "**leaders**" and there are "**finders**." "Leaders" walk into boardrooms having clearly identified the entire gamut of human, financial and infrastructural resource available to them in order to accomplish a given objective. They know precisely where to find it and how to mobilize it. They begin their presentations with "...ladies and gentleman, this is what we HAVE..." "Finders" walk into boardrooms having clearly identified the entire gamut of human, financial and infrastructural resource that is **not** available to them or at their disposal. They stipulate them as indispensable in order to accomplish a given objective and insist that they must be acquired. They begin their presentations with "...ladies and gentleman, this is what we NEED..."

Here is the **deal**, literally! "Finders" identify and articulate "deficiency"-- all that is wrong. "Leaders" identify and articulate "proficiency"-- all that is right.

The beautiful herds of impala, zebra, wildebeast and other prey awaken on the open savannahs of Africa each morning and skittishly communicate their immediate sense of "deficiency." Instinctively they begin an entire day of "process-centric" thinking. What do we NEED this day to simply stay alive? What do I NEED to survive? And so, en masse and with incredible efficiency, they will spend their day accruing, gathering and FINDING what they NEED; but, what of those majestic predators -- lion, cheetah, and that magnificent leopard? Their morning roar is one of "proficiency!" It announces to the world, and more importantly to themselves, that they are back in all their glory with all their own original equipment for a day of "result-centric" thinking. What do I HAVE this day that will get me "client closure?" What do I already possess that will LEAD me to thrive this day?

Until It's Closed, It's Not A Client.

An unpleasant truth it may be, but that's the way it is, the "gospel" as they say down in the South. You can call them anything you want; prospects, prospective clients, possible customers, candidates, propositions, or any of the other words you'll find in sales training manuals everywhere. One thing you cannot call them is a "client." That term is reserved to describe the phase of a relationship that began as a concept and was pursued with total, result-centric thinking, and which has now developed into a transactional relationship. Just as it is with that master hunter, the African leopard, it's not called food until it is hunted and dead! Only then does that leopard have the right to call it a meal.

How does this happen, and what is the analysis of a client obtained, a deal done, a "meal hunted?"

There is absolutely no question about it, whatsoever, that, in the laboratory of analysis of any "closure," be it social, familial or commercial, one will discover that an unobscured vision of a final result was the very first seed planted. It is without a doubt that you will discover, both in your own instance and with regard to others, too, that a total and undisturbed relationship with an end result was the factor responsible for the movement of an initiative from concept to closure. The singular thing that kept the deal, the idea, the concept on track and prevented it from being swallowed by "process" and pronounced "dead on arrival," was result-centric thinking -- an unwavering commitment to the end result of what you knew initially would be a process. Please follow me carefully here; this is the precise place where so many great concepts are buried and perhaps the leading cause of small business failure. It is critical to understand that, from the moment an idea is born, and until it reaches fruition, it is in the realm of process. Only if it is handled with "result-centric thinking," will it stand a chance of survival. As soon as you are no longer envisioning a result, you have, by default, engaged in process. Process is not an evil thing -- in fact, just the opposite; it is essential and necessary as a delivery mechanism of any result, but it is by no means, at all, the result itself! So often, entrepreneurs, organizations, corporations and the individuals within blur this line and confuse the process of achieving results for the very result itself.

For a leopard in the bush lands of Africa, this would spell certain death for itself and its progeny. In the concrete jungles of commerce, while it takes a little longer for the consequence to trickle down, the very same is so. If we are hunting "process" rather than "results," we will have "concepts" rather than "closure" -- and closure is the thing you want -- a client, signed, sealed and banked! Concepts, on the other hand, are just that! So, you see the problem; if you're a leopard, you can't eat "process."

It is an immense challenge for leaders, entrepreneurs and business managers in today's environment to focus in on what is going to achieve a result, as opposed to what is going to further feed the process. However, this is truly what distinguishes "closers" from "supposers" -- you know, business people that spend their lives saying: "Suppose we…" Taking prospects and potential customers from concept to closure is what is going to feed me and my family!

Make A "You" Turn!

So much was coming at me -- I had so much to learn and know -- there was so much that was foreign to me in the way business in general, and the diamond business in particular, were done in the United States of America. I was faced with adapting to, and understanding, an entire culture.

It was all so different. Perhaps, one of the biggest frustrations was the confusion people would exhibit when I would share this. After all, I am English speaking – what's the problem?

After having lived in South Africa all my life, it was extremely trying and difficult to uproot, at age 30, from all my family, friends, infrastructure and beloved Africa. It was not so much the limited resources with which I was working (i.e. $860.22), it was the magnitude of the responsibility and commitment I had undertaken to provide and manage for my wife and four beautiful children – without a "bloody clue" (as they say in South Africa) as to how this would, in fact, happen. It was an enormously tough period for me, during which I had to literally relearn social norms and societal behaviors that simply were not part of my psyche. But, make no mistake; I had a game plan and a very specific mission statement that read as follows:

Get up early. Pray. Believe that I am designed to succeed. Sell loose diamonds to retail jewelers. Get paid. Pay my supplier in South Africa, and provide for my family on the profit. Be a source of support to the world around me with anything left over. Thank G-d, love life and choose to be happy.

It worked. But, there was one condition and hitch! The "law of nature" would not allow me to diminish, embellish or otherwise alter that original founding credo, not even an iota! I was not allowed to confuse it at all. My human instinct to complicate and confuse continually had to be reeled in and admonished for wanting to "mess" with my success path.

You see, over time, as I started to succeed, part of my daily "to do "list was to prevent myself from sabotaging myself. This entailed a strong dose of discipline to prevent, at all costs, any desire on my part to tamper with the clarity that my original formula and mission statement offered me.

Every day, I would get out there and start hustling, while my subconscious went to work planning and scheming sophisticated war games against "Kivi." It would use everything it had at its disposal: media, politics, economy, society, religion, technology, consumerism, "what if," "should've," "could've," family and money -- all of them were called in as Weapons of Mass Confusion! And, they did a fantastic job, continually gnawing at me to derail from my focus, from my mission objective and, most importantly, from the simplicity and clarity of my mission.

This became my single biggest competitor "predator." Staying attached to **me** and to the simplicity of my mission was the thing that held the key to the success of all my efforts with regard to price, product, service, marketing and strategy. I began to viscerally understand that **I** am my market differentiator, and that **I** am the tipping point of my own success or failure. This did not mean that I did not need the help and assistance of others -- not at all. This did mean, however, that, while there was much that could dictate my success, there was only one thing that could dictate my failure -- and I was looking at it every morning in the mirror!

Friends, here is the discovery of Positive Predatory Pillar No. 1-- Know What **You** Are.

Failure is not the opposite of success. Society suggests that it is, but it is not! According to the Oxford English Dictionary and Thesaurus, the more accurate and appropriate antonym of "success" is, in fact, "**not success.**" This is entirely accurate. Succeeding, or not succeeding, at something is determined, in large part, by all sorts of outside forces and parameters -- contributing factors that are truly outside of one's influence: market conditions, consumer trends, acts of G-d, etc.

For example, investing one's money with corporations like Lehman Brothers or Bear Sterns that have performed for over one hundred years was, by all accounts, considered "successful." However, in the afternoon of a given morning in November, 2008, this was now, by all accounts, considered "not successful." See what I mean?

However, failure-- or its true opposite, achievement-- is determined almost exclusively by its user; meaning that, whether or not something achieves fulfillment or fails is almost entirely determined by the commitment an individual, entity or corporation makes to attaching itself to its founding principles and mission statement. Ask Colonel Sanders of the KFC franchise or a zillion other people you know. The only, and I mean **only**, thing that will derail a user and prevent it from "achieving," rather than "failing," will be its detachment from itself, from its core beliefs and from its fundamental adherence to the very purpose of its existence in the first place. It will self-destruct only if it takes leave of the simplicity and purity of its founding "self!" (The United States of America – please take note!)

For many years, while building my diamond business in America and beyond, many things came and went including clients, suppliers, vendors and money. One thing did not go, and, to this day, remains the same: As long as Kivi Bernhard is attached to Kivi Bernhard and all that that entails, everything else falls **into place**. The moment I confuse this concept with "important detail," everything else falls **apart**.

And so, friends, my internal "self-help library" called on me to develop the first Pillar of Positive Predatory Thinking TM – No. 1: Know what **you** are! -- Take all of **you** to the market and to your workplace -- **you** are your market differentiator! You see, while we go through all kinds of machinations and mental gymnastics -- you know, all the "should we," "could we," "would we," "how," "what if," "when," etc., -- well, leopard haven't got a damn clue! What I mean to say is that leopard, instinctively, are so attached to themselves, their tooling and their apparatus that, veering away from the precision and perfection of their original and "natural" mission statement, they know, will get them killed: "Hunt or Be Hunted!"-- no confusion, no detraction, no embellishment. Nothing that they might hear or see on The Oprah Winfrey Show will influence that one way or the other; nothing Sean Hannity or The View might offer as a "new" societal standard will encourage a leopard to "change its spots."

In the concrete jungle of commerce, the continual bombardment of incoming information from both the media and the world around us has become more and more difficult to simply ignore. It gets streamed into our heads and hearts through T-line internet that moves at the speed of light and is never-ending. As such, I submit to you that the sheer volume and consistency of it will ultimately make it "Public Enemy No. 1." Here is why: It subliminally and subconsciously disconnects you from yourself. You got it! It asks for your constant attention and leaves literally no room for your very own **self**. It simply drowns out your own original self and mission statement, preventing it from being heard over the noise and barrage of alternative suggestions. It is a constant and continual assault on **you**.

This **it** is a known killer of your **you**, and if **you** want to survive, **you** are going to have to fight **it** with everything **you** have. If you do not, **it will** take **you** down. It really is **it** or **you**. The only weapon **you** have against **it** is **you**.

Never leave home without you!

Chapter 4

No Tree Left Un-Climbed!

Positive Predatory Pillar ™ No. 2

In the bush.

Study Your Market Territory: It is with amazement that we watch the leopard's uncanny ability to study, memorize and take inventory of its territory.

Study your trading market, the significant and the insignificant; it will define your specific opportunity.

ON THE RARE occasion that one is privileged to observe it in the wild, the leopard's behavior is truly an amazing thing to see. With incredible stamina, leopard will study and observe almost every square inch of their defined territory. The first time I saw this in the bush, I did not know what I was observing. I remember asking Lawrence, a game ranger and friend, what exactly it was that this beautiful female leopard was doing. Lawrence was focused and slightly nervous -- and, rightfully so; we were only perhaps 150 feet away and downwind from her. He also knew that she was involved in a territorial and management ritual - a dangerous time to disturb any animal, particularly an African leopard. I, on the other hand, was ignorant of what she was doing and was also carrying our safety weapon, a 30-06 bolt action rifle -- otherwise known in the African bush as a false sense of security. Lawrence, who is an Afrikaans gentleman, slowly turned his mouth to my ear and whispered, "They call it "u'kufunda." I leaned forward and whispered back, "What?" Lawrence leaned back to me, putting his finger over his lips to suggest that we keep quiet, and whispered, "Studying...the Shongaan people call it u'kufunda." I responded with a whispered, "Ah ha!" We both then focused back on the rare sighting that we were experiencing. I hadn't fully processed this natural behavior, but I knew that I was observing a fundamental aspect of the leopard's incredible success and a pillar of Leopardology™. Lawrence and I had a good hour or so trek back to camp, giving me ample time to fully explore this aspect of leopard behavior with a good friend and extremely knowledgeable game ranger. Incidentally, about five minutes out from our camp, we had a sighting of a huge male eland. This is the world's largest antelope; male eland sometimes weigh in at over 2000 pounds. It was another beautiful day in Africa!

It was not only the precision with which it happened, but the tremendous display of patience, diligence and commitment of the leopard that made such an impression on me. That majestic leopard was simply taking inventory and committing to memory the very environment and hunting territory in which she lives -- quite literally every tree, every bush, every thicket, every granite rock and almost every blade of grass. She intuitively knew that every square inch of her territory was a potential staging area for either a "client" closure or "client" retention opportunity. She also knew that the time for her to study her market territory would not be while on the hunt; that would entirely jeopardize her ability to be effective. She knew this and, therefore, invested much of her non-hunting time in this process of studying and taking inventory of her hunting grounds.

As if it were something her mother had told her, she instinctively understood that studying her territory with this kind of meticulousness would give her the cover she would need to remain undetected and unseen by her "client prospect." With exactitude, she knew the lay of the land -- what rock to hide behind and what mopane bush to stand behind. She knew which sentinel tree offered her cover and which fever tree offered her a vantage point. She knew, with pinpoint precision, which "client approach" would afford her more camouflage and cover -- whether moving in a westerly direction versus an easterly direction would be optimal because of its terrain and disguise assets.

Without question, leopard will spend the majority of their study time up in trees. No tree goes unclimbed. It is well known that leopard are remarkable tree climbers, displaying fabulous dexterity and agility, while almost effortlessly ascending 20 or 30 feet up into the tree line. Their drew claws and substantial upper body musculature all come together in making them superb tree climbers. But, leopard have a very specific relationship with tree climbing beyond just the cover and protection trees afford them. It is also their "client holding environment." Yeah - you read that right! It is where they will feed on their "kill," safe from competitor predators, maximizing the opportunity for "client retention" -- if you see what I mean. (More about that later!) As leopard move through their territory studying and taking inventory, they will demarcate it by squirting a unique and individual concoction on a particular rock or bush, a practice often mistaken for urinating.

Additionally, you will see leopard placing a personal signature into a tree trunk or log using their extremely strong drew claw. Beyond allowing them to clean and sharpen their infamous claws, this signature is instantaneously recognizable by would-be invaders and warns them that this territory is taken and well managed. Many trackers have told me that they have seen territorial male leopard identify signatures from as far away as 200 feet. I guess it's nature's version of a "John Hancock."

Later that night, under a starlit sky, while schmoozing around a fire, Lawrence and I spent a long time discussing "u'kufunda" and this unique behavior of Africa's most successful feline predator.

Predatory Freeze.

If you are a guy, it is akin to watching your wife give you those eyes, (that I am convinced women are given during the wedding ceremony), after you've just told her for the first time that you and the boys are playing golf today... in an hour. You know, "the look" that says "Congratulations buddy, you've just earned five days of the silent treatment and three weeks in the dog house!" If you are a woman, well, then, you know exactly what I mean!

It is a fairly common thing to observe in the bushveld with all animals, but with feline predators particularly. Many eco-tourists and visitors to game parks most frequently observe it when viewing lion. It is simply an abrupt "stop, freeze and stare" mode that you will see big cat adopt from time to time. They perk their ears, turning them like satellite dishes to fully capture the incoming sound. Their tails tuck in and all their upper and lower musculature constricts, defining their profiles and giving them stature. Their nostrils immediately flair and remain fixed, allowing them to capitalize on their sense of smell. And, of course, those eyes! With sniper accuracy they pinpoint and locate the source of this incoming information, and, with significantly dilated pupils, they lock in and stare down their visual target.

At this point, they offer no response whatsoever and will remain in this state for 10 to 15 seconds, tops. People assume it is a response to having been startled or alerted of potential danger, allowing them to give their full attention to identifying and verifying the incoming information. While this is so, what many people do not know is that "predatory freeze" is a lot more than just a response; it is, in fact, often habitually initiated when there is no danger or disturbance at all. Leopard employ "predatory freeze" with regularity and do so more frequently and for longer periods of time than lion or cheetah, for example.

There is a significant difference between being an active information receiver and a passive receiver of information. Here is what I have just said: Leopard instinctively know that the chance to gather and take in information is a gift! It is an opportunity to learn and formulate an educated response. It is a chance to prepare and organize that response, rather than fall victim to a knee-jerk reaction of the sub-conscious. This instinctive behavior of "predatory freeze" is a stroke of nature's genius that allows predators to activate all their sensory equipment, integrating it entirely into the information gathering process -- all of it – sight, sound, smell and touch -- all of it showing up for roll call in an instant, fully deployed, reporting for duty. Each one of these senses now has pristine, undisturbed and quiet access to the information source. This allows leopard to make independent assessments and analyses based on their sensory specialization. Each sense will compute this information and report its findings to "central command" with a recommended action plan. Only after all senses have reported in with their findings will "central command" make a final decision and issue an official response. This response may vary from "do nothing" to "grab it by the throat and kill it." The point of intrigue here is not the response, of course, but rather the entire notion of being a "manager **of** information," rather than being managed **by** information."

It is such a fabulous opportunity for us human beings to revisit our entire relationship with news, intelligence and information. We are so bombarded by it that we have totally forgotten that, with careful management, it can become our friend. It can become an asset, rather than a liability. As a survival mechanism, all we want to do is switch it off! But, we have entirely lost the notion that it is there for our usage and management, not vice versa. "Predatory freeze" happens in total silence – on purpose! In the first instance, any vocal response, given before all the "intel" is in, contravenes the rule of waiting to respond until all the information is gathered and processed. Secondly, the silence that accompanies this "predatory freeze" is also of an internal nature. It is a silencing of the brain and all the noise it insists on providing, when one is trying to think. It is an entire **body** shut down, so that there can be entire **body** participation.

What a concept – the idea that what gets communicated to me, and what informs me, is not what elicits response in me. I am a chooser, not a consumer. I respond and react only after all my sensory equipment has reported back to my "central command," only after I have processed these reports through my human faculties, thereby generating an appropriate and prudent response! That is the opportunity of information! It is to be chosen, not consumed.

I Ain't Sleeping, Buddy!

It was very cold and the air was thin but full of Africa. I awoke from a heavy sleep to a couple of taps on my shoulder from Lukas, my friend and tracker. It was 3:45 am, and we were moving out. We were supposed to do this only at 4:00 am! This was our last morning in the bush, and we had to make a 200 kilometer trip to Lukas's home village near the town of Makhado, where his wife and sister would join him on a visit with their "sangoma," the witch-doctor. Lukas and his brother-in-law were having a dispute regarding a small parcel of land held by the family, which they both used to graze their cattle. The witch-doctor was going to settle this matter by throwing the bones, a traditional divining ritual that several African cultures have used for generations. Lukas was very distracted by this important event and was keen to make sure that we had plenty of time to make the journey to his village and get to the "sangoma" on time. We had basically broken down camp the night before, and, outside of final pack-up and sweep, were ready to roll.

We had already had a wonderful four days in the bushveld with some magnificent sightings of elephant, buffalo, lion, rhino, wild dogs and a slightly-too-close-for-comfort encounter with an African python, an exquisite non-venomous constrictor that takes no prisoners... but, no "ingwe" (leopard). Oh, make no mistake; it was not for lack of effort; we simply had just not been blessed to see our leopard - or so we thought!

It was now maybe 4:10 am. I did a final sweep of our camp site, while Lukas took the last of a leftover two liter water container and dowsed the slightly smoldering coal and ash from last night's fire. As he stamped his foot into the blue/gray dust-sand to be sure that there were no hot spots, I could smell that pungent but "got-to-love-it" smell that wet embers and coal give off. Mix that with half past four in the still pitch dark morning deep in Africa, and you've got yourself a wakeup call that not even the Ritz Carlton can top! I racked my safety rifle, climbed into the driver's seat of our jeep, and started looking at the area maps for our best route out to meet the tar road about 110 km west of where we were. When Lukas got to the jeep, he stopped right in front of the left front headlight and knelt down to the ground. All I could see now was the dispersed light from his small flashlight. I leaned out the window and asked him, in Afrikaans, what he was looking at. He signaled to me to come take a look. I knew this was something good but was not expecting what came next. I walked around the front of the jeep and knelt down to see what it was that Lukas still had his torch pointed on. Lukas just said, "ingwe" (leopard). He was pointing to a huge, and I mean huge, "spoor" (foot print). He looked at me while he explained that this was a very fresh print of a large male leopard, which he thought might be on the hunt. The print was two or three feet away from the front of the jeep, and we both instantaneously understood what this meant about our safety the night before. Thank G-d for fire! Now folks, I know many of you are familiar with that adrenalin rush you get after buying a triple espresso at Starbucks on your way to the airport, while trying to make a 6:30 am flight. Right? Well, this had that licked tenfold! Lukas stood up and said, "hamba gatle" (let's go). I jumped into the jeep, while Lukas jumped onto it, standing on the top of the engine hood. He made a panoramic study of our location, even though it was still dark, and then took a moment to establish the wind direction. He pointed me to the dirt trail road we were near and sent me in a northern direction. Lukas knew this area particularly well; he had worked several years here for the South African military as a tracker with an anti-poaching unit. (That's another entire book.) My blood was pumping, and I was in my element. We were hot on the fresh trail of Africa's most successful predator, and I felt so blessed to be alive. I was kind of hoping to stay that way, so I made sure to really pay attention to my surroundings and to remain alert but calm. This was our leopard that we had been attempting to find for the last four days.

We had not driven 200 feet from our camp, when I heard Lukas's hand gently but firmly smacking down on the side of the jeep. In bush talk that means, "Stop!" I did. Still working with a Dollar Store issue flash light, Lukas turned to me, while pointing out to his side, and whispered, "Do you see your leopard?" I leaned over to his side and said nothing, as I did a survey of my three o'clock. Lukas was quiet, and I could see that he was trying to get a brighter, more focused beam out of his torch, all the while straining his neck in an attempt to see what he had spotted. I whispered an offer to Lukas of a pair of binoculars. He turned to me and said "I have binoculars in my eyes, but I need light." I reached behind me into a backpack and gave Lukas a megawatt spotlight that changed everything. Ten seconds later, while looking through a pair of binoculars, I just said to whoever was listening, "You are absolutely kidding me!"

It was magnificent! Set back about 150 feet from the dirt road, maybe 20 feet up on an extended branch limb of a large Tamboti tree, there he was! Spread along the entire length of this tree limb lay this superb specimen, collapsed as if he'd had a hard day at the office, fast asleep. It was an incredible sighting, because it was almost entirely unobstructed. What I could not get over was how on earth Lukas had seen it in the dark from that kind of distance. He answered me, "I have binoculars in my eyes." Lukas kept the powerful light just off the leopard, so that it would not irritate this huge cat or cause it to wake. The terrain was way too rough for us to get off road and get closer with the jeep. I looked at Lukas, turned to grab our safety rifle and said, "Come on, let's go," as I quietly began to open my door. Lukas, a tracker who had encountered lion charges and black mamba attacks, gave me a look and a traditional tongue click, accompanied by a single shake of his head, before turning to continue watching our "ingwe" (leopard). I received his message loud and clear. If the situation went south on us, we would literally not stand a chance on earth. Everything was stacked against us. It was dark; it was thick bushveld; it was up in a tree with the advantage of height; and, it was an active time of day for predators of all sorts. But most of all, it was asleep. Lukas turned back to me and reminded me of an old African bush wisdom: "Leopard are wide awake when they sleep."

It is not an insomnia problem, or the fact that they are light sleepers -- not at all: Sleeping, and being perceived by others as being asleep, is a major "territory study" opportunity. Even when they are seemingly sleeping, leopard are actually involved in a sub-conscious process of inventory taking and market study. They are establishing the weight bearing capacity of tree branches and limbs to see if they will hold them and their "client." They are taking note of wind conditions and cover that the particular tree may or may not offer. They are studying passing traffic, both predator and prey. They are also establishing whether the "neighborhood" works for them, and whether they can work in this "kitchen," so to speak. (i.e. Who else lives in that tree?)

It took us a good ten minutes to notice the remains of an impala that was swung over a tree limb opposite our sleeping beauty. We stayed exactly where we were and were privileged to spend the next 45 minutes or so watching this beautiful and powerful, silent hunter-- as outside visitors learning about his world. Lukas was incorrect. He said "fresh print of a male leopard hunting." He was wrong... it had already hunted!

That leopard is not asleep.

G-d, Please Excuse Me While I Urinate On Your Tree.

We touched on this before -- that leopard continually mark and demarcate their hunting territory. They do this with their claws, saliva and most specifically by spraying a personal substance from a gland under their tail. In point of fact, they are not urinating -- it just looks that way. However, this is what they are doing. They are leaving a tangible trail in their "market territory." They are essentially placing a "leave behind" or interactive "business card" for both internal and external competitors. It is just as important for them to message other leopard that they are active in a territory as it is to message lion, cheetah, hyena, wild dog, caracal, etc.

Practically, it allows them to literally map out and define their "market territory," clearly benefiting their own efforts as regards "planning," "client relationship maintenance" and "business development." However, beyond all this is a fundamental cornerstone of individual efficiency and efficacy -- a truly insightful leadership and management tool that dramatically increases one's close rate. Leave a tangible trail. That's it! As you move through your market, leave a tangible trail that simply says **you** were there. This is huge. The principle behind it is concise but extraordinarily profound. It is simply this: What asset is selling you, while you are elsewhere selling yourself?

That asset is whatever tangible trail you have left behind in your market place. While Leopard are actively in pursuit and on the hunt seeking "client closure," the plethora of tangible trails they have left all over their "market territory" are telling their story to others, and, by so doing, relieving obstacles and barriers that will make their next "client approach" just that much easier. For the leopard, it keeps other territorial male leopard away; it keeps other female leopard (possibly in estrus) away; it suggests to other apex and base predators that perhaps they should try elsewhere -- it simply advertises their market presence for them. It's brilliant! Have something sell you, when you are unavailable to sell yourself -- because you are busy selling!

The leopard's tangible trail broadcasts to its "market" that **a leopard lives and works here!**

Home Is Where You Sink Your Teeth!

I was once with my long time bush friend Howard, spending a few days in the Kruger National Park, South Africa. We were in the Shingwedzi Camp, where a good friend of mine was the chief game ranger and guide for the bush walks and game drives. He was excited to catch up with me again, and we spent a good portion of the night yapping, etc. The next afternoon, I saw him in the camp reception office, as he was signing out a rifle, getting ready to take a group of Japanese tourists on a sunset bush walk. It was around 3:30 pm, and Howard and I were just getting ready to head out on a game drive. As we were walking out, my game ranger friend shouted out to me in Afrikaans, "Hey Kivi, why don't you come with me on this walk…it's a 'lekker' (nice) walk near the banks of the river that feed the Kanniedood Dam." I looked at Howard, and we said, "Sure!"

I know I have you psyched for another good bush story, but, unfortunately, I am here to share with you that it was an extremely uneventful bush walk. Yeah, it was Africa and the bushveld -- and difficult to go wrong with just that – but, beyond a few "zeebs" (zebra), "imppies" (impala) and some beautiful bird life, we truly did not see much at all. The visitors were in their element, loving the thrill of being exposed to the potential danger of African wildlife. My friend did a lot of nature explaining, making the tourists' walk a fascinating learning experience. At one point, we were all gathered around a massive termite mound, which was no longer active. After checking it out for snakes, which love to move into old termite mounds, my friend climbed on top of it. One of the many interesting facts that he shared about termite mounds was how leopard will use them for cover and often as a vantage point to spend time observing prey. From a slight distance, the tawny colors in their coats perfectly camouflage them, causing onlookers to think that they are just an extension of the mound.

One of the Japanese visitors, clearly intrigued by this information, asked my friend the following question: "Why would the leopard sit and watch, when there is prey that he can go and catch? Why doesn't he just hunt it, if he can see it?"

My friend turned to me, knowing that leopard are my "thing," and asked if I wanted to chime in with an answer. I smiled and said to the group that the question was a good one. I then offered the following answer: I explained that leopard have a vested interest in the well-being and success of their "clients." If their prey are healthy, the leopard are healthy. In other words, by spending a little time not hunting, but silently observing that their prey are finding water and food and are successfully reproducing, leopard are, in fact, prudently taking the first steps in ensuring their own next meal. If things are working out for their prey, they are working out for the leopards' next hunt! Part of successful and consistent hunting is being cognizant of a successful and consistent food source to hunt! There is an implicit respect that all apex predators display for the healthy viability of the antelope herds that feed them. After all, having well developed canine teeth and impressive jaws is all well and good. But, if you have no healthy antelope necks to sink those teeth into, what good are they? Therefore, often when they are not hunting, leopard will find a vantage point, like a termite mound, and simply "check in" with the herd, scanning for young, old, sick, injured, underfed, overfed, etc. This is the leopard's version of asking clients, "So, how are things going?"

This takes a degree of maturity, business sophistication, discipline and vision that we humans are often not accustomed to providing our clients. The payoff, however, is substantial in many areas, as we will explore when we shift to the boardroom in the next chapter.

This little exchange in the bush was not only fun, but it actually got me a speaking engagement with a subsidiary of the Mitsui corporation for whom this Japanese gentleman worked. I thanked my ranger friend by buying the ice cold "Lion Larger" beer that night.

Chapter 5

Leaving the Comfort of Your Office Chair...for Results!

Positive Predatory Pillar ™ No. 2

In the boardroom.

Study Your Market Territory: It is with amazement that we watch the leopard's uncanny ability to study, memorize and take inventory of its territory.

Study your trading market, the significant and the insignificant; it will define your specific opportunity.

I WAS IN a place many of you know well! I was generally moving in the right direction, making progress slowly and reiterating in my head one thousand times a day, "Rome wasn't built in a day." Well, that's correct, it wasn't, but it was destroyed, virtually overnight, and I just could not find that market penetration and client capture that we all look for when trying to build sustainable business. The jewelry industry is always in flux and rarely has any real consistency that one can quantify, but I was not looking for volume as much as I was looking for a "client base." I was struggling to find that small nucleus of regular, repeat clients that allows us to feel like we have a "business" and loyal client base, small as it may be. I felt that I was taking three steps forward and two steps back; "hunting" clients, getting in front of the loose diamond buyer or store owner; selling **me;** doing some business; then, being thrown back to that empty place we entrepreneurs call, "unemployed until you do something about it."

"But, Do what?" became my question. I was hitting those phones day and night like a man possessed. I was networking, marketing and targeting the full gamut of my client opportunities;   retail jewelers, wholesale dealers, manufacturing jewelers and private jewelers. I was getting up and into my office early with fresh, original and energized marketing ideas and campaigns – And, not only that! I was actually making them happen and getting them out to my clients; discount programs, terms offerings, free delivery, exchange programs, "win a free trip to South Africa and see a diamond factory" promotion, etc. Hey, I was competing, and I was competitive. I was getting lots of recognition for my "clever" marketing efforts, but it just was not converting into regular business and sticking! I began to wonder who was not in my net. What potential client was I not reaching out to, and why was I not getting the sense that I was building a viable and sustainable business? Why was my market seemingly not "getting" that, "I was there, and there to stay!" Hello???...

One Wednesday morning at around 9:15 am, I was meeting a client at his store in Shadyside, Pittsburgh, Pennsylvania to personally deliver a stone that he was due to show his customer at an early morning presentation. Ten o'clock in the morning is early in the jewelry business. I met him in his store, still closed to the public, and consigned him the diamond, while we had a short relationship building "schmooze." I wished him luck in selling the diamond to his customer and headed out. Now, here is a trick of the trade. Security trained diamond dealers know that they should always take different directions in going to and from the car or office; just in case one is being watched, it will confuse and deter the criminal. So, as I left this jeweler, I made my way back to my car in an entirely different direction that took me down the road, right past a small coffee house. Enticed by the aroma, I stopped to grab a cup of "joe." Being a busy time for the coffee shop, there were several people ordering and waiting for orders to be filled. A young lady took my order and asked me for my name to write on the cup. I spelled out "K-i-v-i." I stepped aside and went to wait for my drink. The gentleman next to me looked at me and said, "So, **you** are Kivi! It's good to put a face to that very unique voice." I looked at him, extending my hand, and said "A pleasure to meet you?" He identified himself as Jeff Nalley (not his real name), the proprietor of a major, upscale retail jewelry store in the area. This was a significant account that was now in its 110th year and fourth generation. Jeff was the father of the current store manager with whom I had made contact several times. It was clearly an account I had been "hunting," and, while I had made contact and met with his son, I had not been successful in actually transacting business with them.

I immediately understood that I had an opportunity here and asked him for a moment to introduce myself to him more fully. Once we grabbed our drinks, we moved aside and took a spot to share an exchange. Jeff was an extremely refined gentleman and prominent member of the business community in that area. He took the lead with the following remark: "I have heard your name from my kids and our jewelry buyer, and I have seen your card around the store – but, I have not seen you in the store."

Upon hearing what he had just said, a flash of insight shot through my head, but I did everything I could to remain composed and fully present with Mr. Nalley. I shared with him a little about my diamond business, playing up the fact that I was local and could dramatically reduce his shipping bills from New York by providing him a local, on-the-ground service. I said to him that I would love to pop into the store when he and his wife were there; I asked when the best chances of that would be. He said, "Now!" Off we went, a few stores down, to their beautiful jewelry store. It was still relatively early for a retail store, and it was quiet, giving me good, undisturbed time and access to the entire family and the store.

I studied them, the store, their inventory, their staff, their promotional material and their history. Using all my assets in their original pristine state, I transferred all of me to my client with my strongest South African accent and foreign cultural profile. We spent twenty minutes together, maybe three of which pertained to loose diamonds. As I was leaving, I asked Mr. Nalley what his preferred coffee was. From that day on, I would frequently surprise him with a hand delivered cup of his favorite coffee drink. Everything changed with this account. We began doing regular and good business, inside of an implicit trust relationship, which continued for many years.

On my way back to my office, as I processed the morning's occurrence, it all became crystal clear to me. I had been active **at** my market, not **in** my market. In **that** lay the fundamental difference and catalyst I was looking for.

I began to see it ever so plainly: that master hunter, the leopard, consistently and with total regularity, moving through its "market territory," studying every detail of it ever so thoroughly, taking note of even the most seemingly insignificant minutiae, converting gathered information into pointers that would guide it toward successful "client closure." Of course! – I had not been in **front** of my market, responding to client needs, eyeing gaps and client entry opportunity; I was **behind** my market, coming at them from the rear, sight unseen, lobbying in "marketing missiles" and suggestions of my existence for possible consideration -- if they were even to remember me! This was the flash of insight that had shot through my head space as Mr. Nalley said to me, "....but, I have not seen you in the store." I was servicing my business and executing it in the market place, but I was "hunting" my business from an armchair in my office! This was it! This was what I had been looking for to simply get me in front of my business process and progress. This is what began to give me this sense of stability -- that I was actually building a market territory and not just occasionally servicing a client within my market. There is a huge difference -- and leopard know this! They meticulously study their hunting territory and then leave a tangible trail, letting it become known that they were in their market. And so, that is exactly what that cup of coffee became. It would be the tangible trail of my particular relationship with Mr. Jeff Nalley, his children and their guild retail jewelry store. Every time the aroma of a "bold coffee with steamed milk and two shots of almond syrup" made its way through their store, it would broadcast to the entire store: "Kivi Bernhard from Kivi International LLC, loose diamond wholesaler, who is local in Pittsburgh and with whom we have regularly met and engaged in person, is here."

When this second pillar of "Leopardology™, Study Your Market Territory" became incorporated into my daily routine and integrated into my market offering, my market differentiator became crystal clear to me and to my clients. Additionally, there were incidental and secondary benefits that began to emerge and define my business and market edge.

Instead of starting each day office bound, making client appointments in the afternoon, I switched it! I would begin my day way out in the market place at some "off the beaten path," free standing jeweler, fifty or so miles out of Pittsburgh, where I lived at the time. No appointments and no inventory. You got it! Not a single stone to show. I was not there to "hunt" or close. I was there to study my market territory, leave a tangible trail and have it go to work for me. I was there to define my exact client opportunities and their needs. I was there to clarify for myself precisely what need and service opportunity did or did not exist in my client's specific market and whether or not I was able, or wanted, to service it. This entire strategy of getting **in** to my market, instead of getting **at** it, truly became a turning point for my business.

With regularity, I found myself in the right place at the right time. It took no time for me to figure out that it had to do with neither the time nor the place; it was more the law of "nature" at work. Showing up is 50% of the job. I had truly thought that I really was showing up by arriving in my office bright and early, but, I was not showing up in my "hunting territory." In business development, and maintenance of a business, being absent from your market dictates that you will be entirely a responder and not an initiator of client opportunities.

At an old store, a new store, a family store or a corporate store; in Akron Ohio, Steubensville, Ohio, Erie, Pennsylvania, Kittaning, Pennsylvania or Morgantown, West Virginia; that's where you could find me between 1998 and 2002, on any given day, from 9:00 am to 2:00 pm. I was there collating information and probing: observing the store, the street, the block it was on, and the block before it and after it; touching their showcases, eyeing the styles and price points of their jewelry inventory and offerings; noticing the walls and what hung on them; noticing the floors and whether they were carpet, wood or tile. Just like that leopard, you could find me sniffing and smelling, listening and hearing.

Totally caught off guard by the fact that I was not a traveling salesman, and that I truly did not have anything with me to sell my clients, the store owners or managers would grant me face time that my competitors did not receive. This allowed me to gain a substantial understanding of their business and customer profile, while also allowing us to forge personal friendships and business relationships that would determine the premise of our business transactions. A fascinating thing began to happen: Everything around my client became a statement about my client and his business. Observing totally secondary things served to guide me into "client opportunities" and to assist me in managing risk. For example, by analyzing what kind of internal lighting jewelers had in their store, I was able to quickly gauge whether or not they did a regular loose diamond or bridal business. It's very simple: Jewelers who are doing regular and significant loose diamond business understand the value of proper "white" light in the store and are not afraid of the expenditure involved with a professional lighting consultation and installation. It also immediately tips me off as to their knowledge of loose diamonds and their color characteristics. Stores that are doing a marginal or occasional diamond business, perhaps concentrating more on gold jewelry and giftware, would not so readily incur an expense like that.

And, so it was, that, as my commitment to studying my market territory grew, so did my close rate and business volume. I began to see my time out of the office as an asset rather than a liability; I began to value it and to understand that reaching my destination, as well as the route I took, had value with regards my "client closure opportunity." I soon started to take different routes in and out of the same city or town; back roads, state roads and national roads all offered their own tell-tale signs that spoke to a dimension of my clients' market, which in turn, of course, spoke to me about my clients. Being stuck in four feet of snow, on a main street, outside of M&J Jewelers (not their real name), in Girard, Ohio, told me that there was a strong likelihood that the FedEx or UPS guy might just have the same issue. Now, I knew not to offer them guaranteed 9:00 am "next day delivery" in the winter months – what if the snow affected early morning delivery? This had vast implications. Mostly, however, I was now leading my market and not vise versa. I had market intelligence and information. I knew where my clients were and what their store smelled like! Most importantly, they knew me, and they saw me regularly, giving me multiple opportunities to leave behind a tangible trail.

Shhh ...Your Market Is Talking...Listen!

Here is the thing! You cannot do both! What I mean to say is that either you are talking to your market and pitching it, or it is talking to and pitching you! Neither of you will hear each other, if you both insist on talking over each other.

The magic of "predatory freeze" that we spoke about in the previous chapter is that it forces one to become a listener, and, for just one brief moment, to stop selling. Everything about that leopard is entirely and totally still, including the "chitter-chatter" in its own head. It is listening for even the slightest sound and cannot afford to miss it. Its life might depend on it.

We so often sabotage really viable client development and client closure opportunities by refusing to, well, basically, shut the heck up! If we would just let the buyer buy, or the decision maker decide, or the negotiator negotiate, we might be surprised to learn that he will, in fact, do just that. But, somehow, we persist in injecting ourselves into the place of silence, concerned that if we are not actively selling, we are not actively selling. This, of course, is not so. And, our challenge in increasing our efficiency and efficacy as leaders and closers is to make silence our friend. Use it! Do not jeopardize a potential transaction or market study opportunity by "speaking" it away! Listen, fully, entirely – be totally present.

When leopard do this, they are instinctively managing an urge to react. They are allowing the incoming information to tell its own story without any suggestion or flavoring from their own "conscious"

-- "just the facts, ma'am!" This may, in fact, be our biggest challenge as business leaders and entrepreneurs; that is, to be able to listen to and respond to the unadulterated market information we are receiving. I do not mean to "hear" your clients, customers and market place; I do mean to actually internalize, to listen. My father once told me that the reason we have two ears is so that one can do the listening while the other is doing the hearing. The self-leadership opportunity is as follows: Firstly, go into our market territory and study it without the incessant opinion of our own sub-conscious and its attempt to uphold its own agenda; shut off the noise in our very own heads, so that we can actually listen to what the market place is saying, and not what we are saying. Secondly, once we process this information and draw a conclusion (formulate a response), have the courage and conviction to own that information and response, even though it may not reflect the common wisdom or our personal agenda. This takes guts! I have several clients on my book currently that are good, viable, paying clients with whom I have old and strong relationships. Initially, however, industry friends and colleagues told me that they were "small fry," unattractive accounts, and that I was wasting my time pursuing them -- so did my own "chitter-chatter" in my head. But, once I got on location and in their market -- touched it, felt it and smelled it -- my market study told me otherwise. Yeah – I'm glad I did not listen to either my own head noise -- or anyone else's!

The Multi-Tasking Myth.

It might get you killed! Ask any leopard. Instinctively, when they are using any one of their five senses for intelligence gathering, their bodies naturally slow the other senses down. This way, their whole being is involved in that one engagement, maximizing its return and value to the leopard. Now, if you are a leopard, moving through your market on a fine Sunday afternoon, and you suddenly hear something and give out a growl -- while you are still listening for information -- well, you may have just given up your position to an entire pride of lion (not good – lion pride have been known to kill leopard to eliminate competition). Let's revisit that for a moment. It would have, perhaps, been better to fully listen, determine that this was actually not just a single lion or pair, but, in fact, a pride of some 13 lion. It would have been preferable to move swiftly, without a sound, heading upwind to the top branches of a suitable tree to wait it out, while allowing the lion pride to pass through – thus, avoiding a potentially fatal confrontation. So, let's transfer this idea back to our world. Society has convinced itself of the myth that we actually can multi-task effectively. We cannot do two things at once, and certainly not if we intend to do them well. This also applies to our ability to accurately gather information and facts from our market territory. Taking steps to reduce the amount of multi-tasking we have to do, as well as the intensity of it, is truly key to being effective and producing unusually high close rates in our dealings.

What is really amazing is the degree to which we impose this societal ill of multi-tasking on ourselves and then attempt to establish it as the "normative" standard of operation. Yeah, right! Plug the earphones into the Ipod, while you simultaneously finish downloading a list from Itunes, while you synchronize your PDA with your desktop, while you TiVo your favorite show, while you make an amendment to your Outlook calendar, while you instruct your phone to dial "home," while you complete an invitation to join on Facebook, while you email a PDF to a client, while you phone in a lunch order -- all this while you **LISTEN** to a client conference call, as they share with you their fourth quarter projection. It may get you "killed" by your client!

Shut it off. That damn car radio -- it makes noise! Oh, and once we are discussing this, so does that television, internet and newspaper. They create noise in your life. Stay with me here, people. No, I am not living in the dark ages, and, no, I am not an undercover representative from the Amish community or a member of some wacky biblical cult in Texas. I am, however, suggesting that what one allows into one's head, through one's eyes and ears, becomes the originating source of information that will lead one to either choose or consume. I found myself getting into my car, groomed to go, on my way into the depths of my "hunting territory," client focused and "result-centric," when I would then turn on the car radio to accompany me for the one to two hour ride. In an instant, I was gone. I mean that quite literally. In an instant, my **I** was gone. Something else was now demanding the attention of all of my faculties, and **I** could not hear myself think.

What kind of self-worth and value do we place on ourselves, when we are so ready and willing to have unvetted noise rent space in our heads, free of charge?

Just how much is your **I** worth? Surely, it's worth a lot more than losing it to: a magazine for $3.75; or, an entirely free radio talk show host, who sees the world in two colors -- republican or democrat; or, a print newspaper that regurgitates political talking points for whatever party owns their parent company; or, hours of time at the alter of submission to the internet, which, in exchange for your visit, provides advertising space for automobile manufacturers that believe you will not buy motorcars, unless they are advertized with a sexually provocative video of a women in it or on it. What are **you** worth? I do know this: your own voice, uninterrupted and without outside influence, is definitely worth a listen.

It is no coincidence that the words **listen** and **silent**, share the same letters.

It is particularly critical in the world of business. Clarity of vision and a well fleshed out handle on the mission objective are paramount to the success of any entrepreneurial or leadership effort. Many a clever idea, service or product offering has failed with well-funded marketers, not because of a lack of consumer demand or interest, but, rather, because of the inability of its purveyors to remain result-centric and mentally connected to the founding passion and energy of their market offering. In the analysis, it will invariably have been outside noise and a foreign voice, allowed in at no charge, which shattered the prospect of an idea's progression to market. The voice of doubt and disconnection is what shouts out to us from the daily barrage of WMD's (Weapons of Mass Doubt) that assault us through the media and the world around us. While the human mind is indeed G-d's most powerful creation, it is also arguably His most fickle. As convicted, passionate and articulate as we can be when we conceive of ideas or projects, only the slightest hint of doubt can reverse and even destroy the best of them.

If we are to be successful business entrepreneurs who conceive of ideas and then carry them to market, we have to be prepared and ready to combat the many challenges that we will surely encounter as we attempt to do so. Competitors, pricing, quality, service, delivery, funding, planning and business development, to mention a few, will all play their part in serving as obstacles and barriers to entry for your market offering. However, the one thing that is most likely to succeed in taking you and your idea down is **doubt** -- even in the smallest dose!

Business individuals and entities that have persevered against all odds have not done so just with regards to getting back up time and time again -- not at all. More often than not, their getting back up is a function of their being stubborn and has little to do with perseverance. Rather, their perseverance lies in their unique and non-negotiable connectedness to the original voice that gave birth to their idea or project. It is a total refusal to have anything, even the slightest wedge, placed between themselves and their idea. Nothing that suggests even the smallest hint of negativity or doubt is allowed in. It is simply out of bounds and not available for consumption.

This is what we applaud when we admire entrepreneurial perseverance; it is the notion that those individuals or entities have persevered against the path of least resistance that man is most likely to go down; it is the notion of choosing the clarity and power of one's own voice over the voice of doubt and hesitation, despite the fact that that voice is louder, and more people are saying it; it is the notion of sustaining the discipline and restraint required, so as to avoid falling victim to the noise and voice of doubt that bang on the doors of their hearts and minds every moment of every day. Having the perseverance to switch off a radio, put down a paper, get off the Internet, stop a negative discussion with a friend or think a positive thought are what have allowed the ideas of these entrepreneurs to manifest in the world.

It is their ability to instantaneously tap into their vision in its pristine form, thereby evoking the silence and commitment to **listen,** with their entire being, to what they, themselves, have to say.

All in all, the other myriad details that have brought their project to fruition were merely symptomatic of their unrelenting commitment to staying connected to the passion and articulation of the idea in its virgin form. They have persevered against doubt by listening to their own original voice.

It was only at the moment when I had made an unapologetic commitment to this very thing -- studying and listening to my market territory, listening to my own message of courage and conviction, believing in the feasibility and viability of the loose diamond industry and my ability to play in it -- that I had a paradigm shift from entrepreneur to business owner. I had a client base and a market territory.

Leopard do this; they listen intently to their own internal voice and messaging, and, with unequivocal dominance, establish hunting territories, where they enjoy significant "market share." No, it is not just because they do not have a subscription to cable TV, thereby preventing disconnection from infiltrating; rather, it is because the art of listening to themselves is a primordial instinct that society has not yet convinced them to relinquish.

Down Time Is Uptime.

Your market never sleeps. And, even when it does, much like that leopard we saw at four o'clock in the morning, it is not sleeping. Your clients, customers and market territory are continually messaging you with invaluable information; pricing, client condition, client need and client approach information that, if listened to and acted on, can dramatically affect the profitability and close rate of your business. It is a constant flow that simply peaks and troughs at different times of the day, week, month and year.

But, the fact is that there is always intelligence gathering to be done and information to be gleaned, irrespective of the specific time cycle in which we happen to find ourselves in the market place. It's all good! Daytime, nighttime, open, closed, weekday and weekend -- they all offer unique and specific nuances of information that make for very productive market study time.

Once one develops this mindset, any occasion and time in the market becomes an information mining opportunity that can radically increase market success. Because we are human beings, we naturally compartmentalize our lives and everything around us. We have our work mode, our home mode and our community mode, etc. And, we believe that they truly do not have any **business** overlapping each other. This is where we penalize our "hunt" for success. They very much do overlap, and it is, in fact, the fragmentation of our lives that will do us the most damage as we attempt to succeed. We tend to have very much the same attitude when we are in the market, on fact finding missions, gathering information, or at client appointments. We have convinced ourselves that now is not a good time because of "x," and later is not a good time because of "y." Unless the stars are lined up the way we think they should be, we dissuade ourselves from believing that there is any value to be had by getting out into our market. It sounds like this: the store will be closed; he is not there on Mondays; she is not there on Wednesdays; they don't open until 11:00 am; the buyer is overseas; the buyer is in Vegas; the buyer has already bought; the buyer has no money to buy; their customers have no money to buy; I'll just call them. So, now that you have successfully "thought" yourself out of studying your market, you have also fallen into that trap of thinking that market information comes to you in pristine, clearly labeled and convenient packaging. As you know, it does not, and that is why it cannot be bought or acquired. It has to be gained from feet in the market, if it is to be accurate and effective.

Market information is loaded with nuances and small receptors that only trained ears and eyes can pick up. It's **your** client and **your** market. You know it because **you** "hunt" it! Outsiders might perceive the information, however, the ability to process it and make it relevant to your specific "hunt" lies strictly with you. It truly cannot be acquired from PricewaterhouseCoopers, Deloitte & Touche, or your best friend's father's brother-in-law, who was driving past your client's new construction site yesterday. You know what I mean, right? You hold that precious key which will translate the nuances and minutiae of the information gathered; that key is called "relationship." It is nontransferable, which is why nothing can duplicate the "face time" that you spend with your clients in your market.

It's all an opportunity to study: down time, chilling on a Sunday afternoon with friends at a restaurant; picking up a morning paper and a coffee from a local Starbucks; and, driving home from church or synagogue, taking the long lazy route. It all puts you in the market and in front of incoming data, which is the fuel of creativity and originality.

Consider the following examples: taking a stroll with your family through the spring flower show, where you meet a client and his wife, only to learn that she is an avid gardener; taking your kids to the zoo, where you meet a client with her sister and brother-in-law, only to learn that they are moving to Arizona to start another branch of their exclusive designer jewelry store; indiscriminately driving past the public tennis courts on a long, summer, Sunday afternoon, only to notice a client of yours on one of the courts, opposing another client of yours who happens to be some 45 days late on a fairly significant invoice; or, how about accepting an invitation to attend a fine cigar event and literally walking into a substantial prospect that you have "hunted" for two years without yet closing, only to learn that you have a shared mutual interest, and that his birthday is next week!

As you have guessed by now, each one of the above vignettes actually happened to me -- precisely that way. Every one of them resulted in significant client advancement opportunities and enhanced business. I located and acquired a South African protea flower for my client's wife and her garden. I knew she would appreciate it and mention my name to him regularly, becoming a verbal business card. She did! Ever since we offered to assist them with some impressive diamond inventory for their Arizona store opening, our business with both stores has increased. My tennis enthusiast client was most helpful and instrumental in getting me paid by my other tennis enthusiast client. And, it was the $18.00 cigar and the Tennessee bourbon, delivered a day before his birthday, that finally got one of Ohio's premier fine jewelers to pick up a phone to me and connect. We have done business ever since. Down time really can be up time!

Wear Cologne!...And Put That In Your PDA!

Leopard leave a tangible trail behind them. I learned that, if I were to be a serious business person looking to demarcate my territory, define my client base, maximize client contact and increase the ROI of my market study efforts, then I should do so, too.

Now, granted, licking and spraying pavements and sidewalks outside of my clients' stores and offices would certainly resemble leopard-like behavior, but I am not entirely sure it would work -- on several levels. Leaving a tangible trail behind me that would invoke all five senses and unmistakably brand me with my client, however, would work. Beyond that, there would be the function of demarcating my territory for broadcast to my competitors -- a mechanism of nonverbal communication that they would encounter when "hunting" my clients in my territory. There is a critical component that one must understand about human behavior and the entrepreneurial mind.

It works much like that of a seasoned and finessed criminal. It will always take the path of least resistance. In fact, I remember reading in the 1990's about a controlled study that was done in Johannesburg, South Africa, which was, and perhaps still is, per capita, the car theft capital of the world. It was determined, categorically, that the perception of a car, alarmed and equipped with sophisticated, engine disabling technology, was dramatically more valuable in protecting the car than the actual technology itself. If criminals could make a quick, easy and accurate assessment that a particular car was equipped with anti-theft technology, there was an eight in ten chance that they would pick a softer target. It is a primordial instinct all living things share -- head for the path of least resistance.

In business, our competitors do precisely the same thing. If there are quick, easy and accurate indicators messaging potential competitors that you are very much alive and active with a client, they are most likely to pick a softer target. I share with you, by way of example, that I believe that the outside door sticker, notifying customers that a store accepts Visa, MasterCard and Discover, has to be the most effective, ingenious and successful marketing material in the company's history. I do not know this -- I just contend it. Here's why! More so than communicating to potential clients that their plastic is welcome in that store, it unequivocally demarcates their territory and leaves a tangible trail for their competitors that says: "We were here." Try being the American Express point-of-sale representative calling on retail accounts, when, before you even walk in the store, you are "told" that Visa, MasterCard and Discovery are alive and active with the client you are trying to prospect. See my point? What a brilliant use of Leopardology™! Leopard leave a tangible trail that not only messages their prospective "client," but messages their competitors as well.

A year after I had come to the United States, I had to get from Pittsburg, Pennsylvania, to New York City and back. I had the opportunity to meet with a Belgian diamond cutter. My wife and I spent days weighing the decision, primarily because of the cost involved. We simply could not afford the cost of a flight or a train. The only option was an $88.00 round trip fare with the Greyhound bus service. I took it. It was the first time in my life that I had ridden long distance on public transportation; South Africa still does not have much in the way of developed public transportation. Once the deed was done and the ticket was bought, I was keen to engage the experience, though I was bothered by the time loss involved in the 12 hours of travel each way. But hey, this was a unique opportunity to study my market and take inventory of the Pennsylvania Turnpike and every rest stop on it. I was one of the first people on a bus that would take on another forty, or so, passengers and had the pick of the seats. I selected a seat based on what I thought would be most undesirable to anyone else, thinking this would give me leg room and space. I was wrong. The last passenger on the bus was a large-framed man, behind whom they literally closed the door. He stepped up onto the floor platform, scanned the available seats for a moment, and, you got it…placed himself in the aisle seat of my previously unknown three seat haven. I immediately introduced myself and extended a hand shake, which he accepted. He mentioned his name and then communicated in Spanish that he did not speak English. I communicated in an extremely poor Spanish that I did not speak the language. The language barrier, however, was not the problem over the next 12 hours!

Speaking was not the difficulty: Breathing was the difficulty. I mean, just breathing good, old-fashioned air into my lungs was going to be a fabulous challenge. No, no, the gentleman was not a vagrant who was unhygienic and unbearable to sit next to -- just the opposite.

He had spent so much time in the shower, had used so much deodorized soap, and had bathed himself so extensively in aftershave and cologne that I was strongly considering breaking the glass to get air. You have no idea of how this gentleman reeked of some extremely cheap cologne. The reason I know it was cheap is simply that, to use four bottles of it at a time, it would have to be cheap. People were really battling with this, but only one guy got to sit next to him -- Yours truly!

I just kept on thinking how my sister, who is an asthmatic, would have been in anaphylactic shock already, so I guess things could have been worse. An hour or so into the trip, my fellow passenger fell asleep, and that's when I made my move to a much tighter, but more manageable, location. The entire bus, however, was engulfed, and the only benefit the cologne provided was that of masking the wonderful aromas that the toilet at the back offered.

Let's just say that many of us on the bus were praying that we were on a plane, preparing for a crash landing, and hoping for the release of oxygen masks from the bulkheads above us. It never happened, and the only reprieve came from the time we spent outside the bus at the rest stops, breathing in far more manageable and comfortable carbon monoxide from passing trucks.

We made it, thank G-d, uneventfully to New York City and pulled into Time Square at 7:20 am. I headed for a public rest room, where I could freshen up before scavenging for a cup of coffee — to, hopefully, help me find my brain. I had to be in the diamond district by 9:15 am to meet my appointment at a kosher restaurant for breakfast. I felt absolutely awful; I looked like a buffalo and reeked from "eau de Wal-Mart." I was not a happy camper but did what I had to do. The plan was to meet this gentleman, meet some other diamond contacts while in the city and get back to Pittsburgh on an afternoon Greyhound bus -- which I would ride in an unconscious state.

I met the gentleman from Belgium. We shook hands and had a good meeting. The day unfolded basically as planned, but little did I know that it was to generate one of my most successful branding and tangible-trail campaigns, which I still use to this day.

Remember, I reeked of second-hand cologne, and I was also the lucky passenger that got to shake "Mr. Waytoomuch," by the hand. I never got to shower or change before my client meeting.

Several weeks later, I followed up with my Belgian contact, who, of course, was settled back in his home office. It took me several attempts to get him on the phone, but I did, eventually. As I began to reintroduce myself and refresh his memory, he abruptly, but kindly, interrupted me. He said the following: "I know exactly who you are -- I can smell you right now."

We went on to establish a strong and mutually beneficial business relationship. But, it was the power of scent as a branding tool that left its mark on me most. I so clearly observed how this overpowering and somewhat unpleasant second-hand cologne had served as such an effective "leave behind" and tangible trail for my client prospect. I knew that, if I could refine it and reduce it, (to perhaps 1000th of the strength I experienced), that this could uniquely work for me long after I was out of my market place. I started thinking and generating marketing ideas like scented business cards, store air-fresheners, etc.

So, here is what I came up with. I researched and bought a European, not easily available, somewhat obscure, but very upscale men's cologne from Harrod's in London. I used it in very small but present amounts. I began to purchase and wear power shirts that were not conservative and were a little gutsy. I had a buffalo hide belt and a men's attaché bag that was not commonly seen in the USA.

Now, here is where it gets a little, "Ok, this guy is strange..." I would spray my hand with my personal brand cologne and then handle all my gear, belt, pens, pencils, diamond tweezers, business cards, diamond grading cards and marketing material -- on purpose. Everything smelled like Kivi. Ladies and gentlemen, I am here to share with you that this strategy became an integral and indispensable component of my market share penetration. Second only to my accent, (which is why I would leave voicemail for prospects after I had met them), my "scent trail" was a constant seller of **me**, when I was no longer there to sell **me**. It would literally aerate my brand and presence in my market for days and weeks after I had been there. Beyond the visual impact of my marketing "stuff" in their store and the vocal impact of my voice, my scent was broadcasting me and my market offering when I was not there.

It was also letting other diamond salesmen smell my presence.

Study your market territory and leave a tangible trail.

Chapter 6

Why Leopard Attend
Every Trade Show They Can!

Positive Predatory Pillar™ No. 3

In the bush.

Study Your Competitor Predator: I have seen
leopard deep in the bush, or high up from the vantage
point of a tree, watching a lion or hyena hunt unfold
200 to 300 feet away.

Study your competition;
it will define *your* edge
and client approach.

IT WAS SOMEWHERE in the month of April, and it was one of the occasions on which my dream was not a dream. There we were in the bush for four days -- all of us: my wife, my kids, I and my Africa – my dream. Now, while my family share my heritage and my love of African wildlife, they are not quite as "bosmal" (Afrikaans word meaning bush-mad) as I am. They want to be with the family -- in the bush. I, on the other hand, want to be in the bush -- with the family. You see the problem here? So, I have to embrace major compromise on these trips. For example, we have to stay in a game reserve with managed camps that offer beds, electricity, and flushing toilets, etc. We can't do anything "dangerous," and we have to relax with each other in between game drives. Now, as if that is not punishment enough for me, (I mean, it's like giving a kid a lollipop and telling him or her to only lick it some of the time.), my insistence on getting out at 5:30 am with the entire family is generally not well received, if you catch my drift here. But, you do understand that there is no way that I am going to allow the opportunity of the family's being in the bush to fail to be all that it can be. Therefore, getting in the five hours of prime viewing time from five to ten in the morning is not even remotely negotiable. So, every morning at 5:15 am, I hauled those beautiful sleeping kids of mine and my sleeping beauty (quite literally) of a wife out of bed and into our land rover. We were in the Balule Bush Camp of the Kruger Park, and the bush was dry from lack of rain; so was the game viewing. For three days, I "schlepped" my wife and kids out of that deep sleep that is a signature of bush life. We did not see a thing -- I mean not a thing; well, not quite. On the second day at about 7:30 am we saw impala near the river.

However, (and this is where is gets good!), on day four, all that changed in a major way, and we went on to see one of the most intriguing and rare predator sightings I have ever had in the bush. It was maybe 6:30 am, and the family was still waking up, wrapping themselves in blankets, while getting bounced around a little at the back. We were on the Ngotso Road, and, not 50 feet in front of us, on the side of the road in a grassy patch, was a fresh, perfectly intact, fully grown, adult female impala (110 lb antelope) that had been "closed" by, well, someone or something! It was the strangest thing. There was this perfect "client closure" just waiting for profit taking, and there was absolutely no sign at all of anyone around to do so. This was bazaar, to say the least. Ok, I was baffled here, but, now, everyone was wide awake, and our adrenaline was flowing.

Now, I knew there was definitely something big going on here, because nature is precise and wastes nothing. There is also little place for "just because" in the wild. Things do not happen out of context; they are often laden with genius and reason that, many times, is simply not apparent to the human eye. It would turn out that this was just such an occasion. In an attempt to hone their skills and increase their "close rate," big cat, particularly leopard, have been known to kill pray for practice; but, the scene here did not look like this was one of those instances. It was early in the morning, prime hunting time, hunting time for food, not for practice! The location of the kill was also too perfect and did not resemble a teaching opportunity; rather, it appeared like a well-selected and precise "client signing location." This kill was as fresh as fresh gets, and, yet, there was not a single predator of any kind to be seen. Where were all the other players – silver backed jackals, vultures, hyena, etc.? There were simply too many indicators telling me that this was a predatory situation with a fascinating learning opportunity behind it. It was.

All I wanted to do was the illegal and stupid thing - you know - get out of our vehicle and check this whole thing out on foot. It was just us; we had not seen another vehicle out there since we left the camp, and it was 6:30 am, or so, in Africa. Beyond the fact that, in the Kruger Park, I would not have had a safety weapon with me, (it is illegal, as it should be), I wanted to teach my kids that rules are for obeying. However, between you and me, let me just tell you: I really wanted to get out and up-close to examine that carcass for tracking and tell-tale signs that would help me uncover this really strange scenario. I had to resolve to do so from the confines, but safety, of our vehicle. Ok, so I did a little off-roading and reversed up onto a large mud rut.

This was the deal. This was not a lion kill, because, firstly, a young female impala is a good appetizer but certainly not a viable "client selection" to feed a lion pride. Zebra, wildebeest, buffalo or giraffe offer better ROI and are much more appropriate "client opportunities" for large lion prides. Secondly, they would not abandon the kill. It was not a leopard kill, because, although it was a good "client selection" for a solo solitary hunter, it immediately would have been taken to a "client holding environment," into thick grass or cover and then up into a tree. This carcass was lying virtually untouched, fully exposed to all. My gut and head told me that this impala had been taken down by cheetah; it was also clear to see from the chest marks on the impala. Cheetah, who tend to attract attention from other predators with their extremely fast but tumultuous hunt, eat their prey where they have killed it, and do so quickly. In an effort to get straight to the highly nutritious meat first, they typically start with the chest area.

So, this was a cheetah hunt and successful "client closure." But, where were they, and why were they not feeding? I had the whole family on the lookout - north, south, east and west. We slowly drove a kilometer up and down the dirt road, fully engaged, looking for a cheetah sighting.

We found them -- two of them! These beautiful specimens were located on a sand mound approximately 600 feet away from their "client." They were edgy and very active, standing up on the mound, glancing back and forth between us and the site of their kill. Now, I was really confused. We had a really great sighting of these cheetah, just us, alone with these magnificent predators; it was a special moment for the whole family. But, I was intrigued by this entire scenario, and my curiosity encouraged me to go back to the kill. As we reached the impala carcass, now some twenty minutes since we had found the cheetah up the road, I could see that vultures had begun to circle in the air; I then noticed a collection of eight or so lappet-faced vultures perched on a dead tree limb nearby. This was going to get good. After continuing to scan the area with binoculars, I still could not see signs of any other predator that would be keeping the cheetah away from this still warm carcass. We refocused our attention on the closed, signed and sealed "client" that had strangely, but evidently, been abandoned by the "entrepreneurs" that had closed it. What we saw over the next 15 minutes was absolutely and entirely amazing. Three of the largest vultures that had been perched on the nearby tree limb now made their way to the impala. They stood some three feet away and carried out a pecking order ritual, strutting their stuff, which evidently determined some form of dominance among them. After circling around the impala several times, the largest and ugliest of these huge birds began "engaging this client." Now, here is what happened: Within 15 seconds of this, the collection of vultures, (which by now numbered fifty or so), that had been maintaining a holding pattern in the air, suddenly, at once, converged on the ground. With a massive commotion, but with military order, they ferociously commenced a feeding frenzy that I captured on video. Over the next 15 minutes, and in front of our eyes, approximately 70 birds of prey, comprised of five or six different species, went on to consume every single morsel of that carcass; the only remaining evidence of this impala was a white boned skull. Not a thing remained. A Blackbacked jackal showed up-- too late!

Just as the last of the birds was leaving, I could hear a vehicle behind us. It was a game ranger and his guests from Olifants Camp on the morning drive. We quickly exchanged notes, and he could not believe what he had just missed; he was eager to see if at least the cheetah were still there. I could not believe what **I** had missed! He told me that, about 2 kilometers away, they had caught a good but distant sighting of a leopard with its well-eaten kill in a tree. Wham! After a quick "bush-consultation," it all came together. And, so was born a key component and pillar of Leopardology™.

The game ranger knew these cheetah as territorial to that area, as was the leopard. This was their hunting territory and "client market." We extrapolated that, after the cheetah had killed the impala, something or someone (a bird, monkey, etc.) tipped them off and blew the leopard's cover. Cheetah, even in pairs or more, are reluctant to take on a full grown adult leopard and would rather back down. They had, most likely, caught sight of the leopard and were too nervous to begin feeding, choosing rather to wait it out. The leopard did not move in on the kill and challenge the cheetah for the "client," because it was not hunting- - it already had a "client" it was busy with, as the group had seen earlier. The leopard was, most likely, on a "market study" stroll, when it suddenly had an opportunity to do something that leopard often do-- study its competitor predator. There was a stand-off: The cheetah were too uncomfortable to feed, fearing attack from the leopard at any time; The leopard had no intention of attacking, as it was there as an observer to study the cheetah; The cheetah moved off to find cover away from the kill, but still in sight of it; The leopard moved on once the study opportunity was over -- mission accomplished.

Amazing, isn't it? Leopard will exert much effort and time, following from a safe distance or observation point, as a lion, hyena or cheetah hunt unfolds. It allows them to clearly define their specific "market opportunity" and to gain deeper perspective into their "market differentiator." Leopard, at any and every given opportunity, seek to observe their competitors in action and to study their competitors' prey selection, approach, hunt methodology and feeding behavior. They love to attend "trade shows" -- it allows them to observe the "competition."

What a morning that was! – And, my kids are ever grateful that I pulled them out of bed at 5:15 in the morning, while on a safari "vacation."

Who Else Has Whiskers Around Here?

There is a dual process that leopard employ when studying their competition. In the first instance, they need to accurately identify their competitor -- not the competitor they perceive or would like to think they are up against, but the competitor predator they actually compete with; Secondly, leopard then embark on fully studying the hunting methodology of this competitor.

Identifying true competitors can vary from territory to territory where different populations are more or less successful. For instance, in parts of the Kalahari Game Reserve, the famous Kalahari lion has managed to sustain itself, and, as such, is much more of a competitor for leopard than are hyena, which are less prolific in that area. In most other regions, this would be reversed. So, the process of the leopard's identifying its true competitor is not one-and-done (as we say in South Africa). While there may be an instinctive, general and universal awareness that lion, cheetah and hyena compete against the leopard, this is always in flux and can change quickly. Factors such as water supply, river conditions and the well-being of certain herd species can all impact which competitors leave or enter a territory.

However, once leopard have accurately identified their competitor predators within their hunting territory, they go on to spend much time studying the hunting methodology of those competitors. This is an amazing phenomenon that, in its simplicity, offers so much profundity. Staying well back and, hopefully, out of sight, leopard will simply observe a competitor hunt unfold, studying the exact strategies employed. They will bank it to memory and learn from both the efficiencies as well as the deficiencies of the hunt -- what worked well, what did not. Channeling this information into their own hunt allows them to continually improve on their "game," increasing their "closure rate" and decreasing their risk exposure.

Lukas, my friend and tracker, with whom you are familiar by now, has shared with me much about this unique leopard behavior of studying its competitor predators; he refers to it the same way he refers to leopard studying their hunting territory -- "u'kufunda" -- simply, the Zulu word for study. As instinctive as it is for leopard to do this, there is nothing at all simple about it. Lukas told me that, when he was a boy, his father once took him to the chief of their home region in the Makhado/Musina mountain range for a certain cultural initiation ceremony. He told me that he and his father were to spend two nights in the chief's village, excluding the day and a half foot travel in each direction. This was an important and joyous occasion during which he would receive general guidance and what was described to me as a specific life statement from the chief that could guide Lukas into his teenage years. He told me of this event and spoke of it with very fond memories -- the ceremony, the dancing and the food. Ten or so other boys had also arrived with their fathers, and, on the second day, in private audience with the chief, they were each given specific "iseluleko" (advice). This advice was particular to each young boy and apparently spoke to their specific physical and mental make-up, as well as their moral constitution.

Lukas explained that, when he and his father came before the honored chief, the chief greeted them warmly and immediately began speaking. After spending some time on generalities, the chief placed his hands over Lukas and looked him straight in the eyes. Lukas paused for a moment at this point, almost as if he were transporting himself back to that moment in time. He said that he remembered the chief's looking deep into his soul, when he gave him his "iseluleko." I asked Lukas if it was okay for him to share with me what he had been told. He smiled at me and said that it was, and that the following was what the chief had told him:

... You must study life, the people, the animals and nature – but, not like the African vervet monkey that is impatient to stand still long enough to learn. No, you must study like the leopard and use much patience to watch, see and study your friends and your enemies; know them well and study their behavior. This will keep you safe and make you successful...

Lukas then said to me that, as of that point in time, there have been few problems and situations in his life that he has not been able to successfully resolve by simply taking the time to fully study the facts, the players and the options.

As leopard study their competitor predators, they: A) spend the necessary time to be fully confident that they have identified their true competitors, and B) allocate sufficient time, effort and energy to studying their competitors in action in the field, quite literally.

One Lion's Poison Is Another (Leopard's) Meat!

Competitors are not "one-size-fits-all." This is true of all life's pursuits and achievements. There is not just one, singular, definitive rule of thumb when it comes to success; things are achieved in different ways by different people. The only common thread that all who succeed will share is the result-centric thinking we spoke about earlier, along with an unwavering and determined commitment to their project. Something that one will discover from an interview with any number of "successful" people will be the variety of obstacles they have encountered, not the absence of them. What posed as a major competitor for one entrepreneur did not even feature for the other and vice versa. Here is the critical thing to wrap your head around: Just as G-d has designed you with precision, so, too, has He designed your "competitor." The two of you are perfectly matched for each other, and, upon closer inspection, you will discover that, in fact, you both hold secrets to each other's success.

We need to stop for a moment and recognize this; we need to placate the fear we have that drives us to "hate" our competition, and actually entertain the notion that they are an asset, not a liability. Leopard, more so, perhaps, than any other predator on earth, have internalized this instinctively. As such, they truly value the opportunity to not only identify their competitors, but to accurately study them in action. Leopard also "get" that each one of their competitors has different dimensions of efficiency and efficacy to offer. Part and parcel of this is an understanding that what works for one does not, automatically, work for the other. Additionally, the fact that there is difference not only affords a learning opportunity about one's own hunting methodology, but can also offer unexpected and tangible profits. This is a regular occurrence in the bush, and, I submit to you, in any "hunting" market. Studying your competitor predator can not only translate into better hunting in the future, but can, occasionally, yield a really good meal or snack, right now.

Awhile back, we were bush-hiking along a rock face, midway up a mountain that ultimately fed into a low lying valley. It was late afternoon, and we were being beaten by a scorching African sun. This was our second day here, and we had been trying to follow a leopard spoor (track) that we had caught sight of earlier in the day. The interesting thing was that we had seen the leopard spoor not too far from where we had seen a healthy lion pride numbering some 11 lion, spread all over and lethargically napping in the shade of some trees and thickets. Just before we came across the entire pride, maybe 250 feet before, we had been very fortunate to see two young, female lionesses with a steenbok (smallest of the African antelope) that they had "closed." They were lying in the grass with their "client," but not feeding on it. It was strange!

This rock face was prime leopard territory and just had to be somebody's home. Put it this way – if I were a leopard, that rock outcrop was where I would call Sears to deliver my appliances and Best Buy to install my surround sound and cable TV. It offered all the exact conditions for prime leopard living, and we hoped to get a sighting of the territorial male leopard our tracker knew. While we had the right country, the right location, the right time of day and the right people involved, we did not have the right luck! The majestic and skillful leopard had evaded us again, and the next three hours of daylight did not yield a leopard sighting. In close proximity to each other, the four of us began our way down to the valley, where our jeep would carry us for the 40 minute drive back to our camp. When we got back down to the valley, the sun had already set, and we were working off what I like to call "*eveningnoon*" light, that very distinct mix of the remaining rays of sunset with early radiance of a young moon on a clear evening. A dangerous time in the African bushveld, predators are just beginning their "sales meetings" and planning strategies for the night's "client interactions."

We got back to the four-wheel drive and unpacked our day's gear into it. We were tired and dehydrated, but the opportunity to crack open an ice cold brew in the middle of the African wild was way too difficult to pass up. Besides, our tracker said, let's sit a while and see what moves through the valley. What are you going to say? -- No?

Now, it was evening proper, and our visibility was marginal at best, particularly considering that we were dealing with living things that see better in the dark than we human beings do in bright daylight. We were all sitting on the jeep -- two of us on the top of the engine mount and the others on the roof rack. We were all nursing those now slightly cold beers, while our tracker enjoyed a pipe that smelled like it was filled with elephant dung, but it wasn't. It was rhinoceros dung – just kidding! It was a home grown mix of banana leaves and commercial tobacco, but it did help keep the mosquitoes away. It was incredibly peaceful and beautiful out there, and we were enjoying just being alive, as well as the now fading silhouettes of the two giraffe that were way off in the distance. We sat a while longer and then, staying really close to the jeep, prepared to leave. We hit the lights, including two powerful spotlights on the sides, and pulled off. We had not moved 200 feet and had just gotten on the dirt road that would take us back to camp; I was driving, and it was one of the guys in the back that called, "Stop! four o'clock!" In the bush, as in the military, one of the best ways to quickly describe a location is to use the dial of a clock as a reference point. So, assuming that twelve o'clock is directly in front of me, four o'clock would be behind me on my advanced right hand side. I stopped, and we all swung around to see the spotlight perfectly illuminating a magnificent nocturnal sighting.

There was our leopard, frozen, looking at us in the 4x4. It stared at us, taking in information about this big strange "animal" with bright lights that makes a low but grinding noise. In its mouth was a steenbok -- not any steenbok, as our tracker pointed out – but, the exact one that we had seen earlier that day in the possession of those two lionesses. He stared a short while longer and then carried on into the grassland, heading straight for the rock face we had left not 40 minutes ago. We caught a glimpse of his swaying but powerful back once or twice, but that was it. Our tracker turned to us and said "...daytime, maybe, but to follow him on foot at night is a death wish..." I took my foot off the clutch, pulled into the center of the dirt road, and, before stopping the jeep, turned around and said, "Nice one, buddy...good spotting." Then, we regrouped for a moment, and deduced the following.

That steenbok, a 12 pound antelope at most, was absolutely the same animal those two lionesses had caught earlier that day. Here is the deal. There is very little a small 12 pound antelope will do to feed a pride of 11 hungry lion. But, if you, as a lone sub-adult lioness, are found by other members of the pride (most importantly by the alpha male) not to be a team player, taking care of your own hunger, you might well pay with your life. You certainly cannot show up with it back at the pride, because a major war will erupt. As well, you cannot take the chance of sneaking off into the grass and eating alone, because you will get caught and killed by the pride. So what you do is abandon the kill and live another day to hunt with the pride. Our leopard, most likely hidden by the cover of treetops, perched on a branch, observing his competitors as he often does, watched these lionesses hunt this steenbok. He sat there, knowing that sunset would be the announcement for the lionesses to join the pride. They did exactly that and abandoned the steenbok, so as to spare themselves the wrath of the pride.

Because of the leopard's instinctive commitment to **study its competitor predator**, it found itself in exactly the right place, at exactly the right time. In the cover of dark, using its specialized equipment and characteristics of stealth and silence, it descended the tree and claimed the abandoned steenbok. Beyond yet another opportunity to learn from and study its competitor predator, doing so actually gained this leopard a tangible and immediate "client opportunity."

Chapter 7

Competitors... It Pays Big Money... To Love Them!

Positive Predatory Pillar ™ No. 3

In the boardroom.

Study Your Competitor Predator: I have seen leopard deep in the bush, or high up from the vantage point of a tree, watching a lion or hyena hunt unfold 200 to 300 feet away.

Study your competition; it will define *your* edge and client approach.

My late Grandfather, Sydney Neuman, spent his

entire life and his working career in the United States of America, calling on retail accounts for three renowned paint manufacturers including the great Benjamin Moore Company. He successfully sold paint to hardware and home improvement stores across northeastern America. He did this with passion and extraordinary honesty for more than 48 years and built an international reputation as a "gentleman's gentleman." Just ask his headstone! He knew only civility and truth, and that both of them paid well! After my grandmother passed away, my grandfather joined us in South Africa, where he lived out the remainder of his years. I was too young and arrogant to fully appreciate the astonishing bastion of work and life experience that lay deep in this gray haired man, but, in spite of myself, there were several seminal moments that I shared with him in private time. Each one of those "chats" has turned out to be priceless – each one a moment during which those invaluable pearls of wisdom are handed down from one generation to another -- the real stuff of life and the secrets of its success that don't make their way into the textbooks.

On one occasion, he was sitting outside, enjoying the South African sun in my mother's beautiful garden. I joined him with a glass of water and asked him to share with me what he thought was the single biggest detractor, and conversely, the single biggest contributor, to his sales success across a career that spanned half a century. After I repeated the question for his failing hearing, he looked at me and drew me in close. In a rhetorical manner he asked, "You do mean besides the work it takes to be honest and polite?" He then replied directly to my question saying, "The guy from the Pittsburgh Paint & Glass Company." I looked at him asking for clarification. He shared with me that, throughout his career, competitors in the paint industry came and went. However, there was a sales representative from the Pittsburgh Paint & Glass Company, whom he knew well, even socially, who was his most significant competitor. He then paused a moment and offered just a short cryptic explanation as follows: "I studied his every move... sure he cost me sales, but he made me many more!" I had gotten it, and I understood well what my grandfather had just handed me. He went on to tell me that, at industry trade and exhibition conferences, which were certainly not what they are today, he would often spend most of his time spying on the Pittsburgh Paint & Glass Company booth, studying the comings and goings of its visitors, etc. He said to me that all the other salesmen were so busy with their **customer** appreciation gimmicks that it gave him ample opportunity to be busy with **competitor** appreciation and study time. Little did I know that this would become reinforced for me by my observation and amateur study of leopard behavior, becoming a pillar of Leopardology™.

Competitor Appreciation Day!

It's true! We are so hung up on this "client appreciation" stuff. There are vendors that cater exclusively to this market; corporate gifts, food baskets, widgets, gadgets, gizmo's and stuff, designed to express your appreciation for your client or customer. My question is this: When was the last time you sent a box of chocolates to your most "valued" **competitor**? Now make no mistake, "Klients are King." I get that and encourage the notion that we appreciate our clients. But, follow me here. There is major reward and benefit to be had by changing the way we view our business competitors. It's a paradigm shift, but I share with you that, where client appreciation days will actually cost you money, competitor appreciation days will make you money.

As a pillar of Leopardology™ for many years now, I have instituted in our diamond company that April 1st is officially "competitor appreciation day." You got it! Fools day – the joke is on my competition, not knowing that they afford me tremendous marketing and client approach opportunities. It's a little counterintuitive, but you would be amazed as to what ideas, strategies and business projects are generated from this day of dedication to studying our competitors. We all come together after having been allocated specific competitors to research. Throughout the course of the day, my office staff and I will present an overview of each of our most significant competitors, their market offering and an actionable market engagement we can implement as a result. Just as with the leopard, it is a two phase process. In the first phase, we make sure that we have identified a true competitor -- an entity that we are meeting on the mat of "sales competition," out there in the jungle of commerce, offering similar categories and similar deliverables to our company. The second phase is the process of studying that competitor; its market offering, its website, its web presence, its literature, its marketing material and its market perception. It is studying: what that competitor hunts, and how he hunts it; what terms he offers; what services he offers, and how; what the organizational structure is with which he operates; whether there is a disconnect between the top and the bottom (Meaning, are their CEO's salespeople that are, themselves, involved in the "hunt?"); who or what answers his phones; whether he can deliver what he has promised; and, what your shared clients have told you about his market offering.

Amazingly useful and insightful information and intelligence are gleaned from our competitor appreciation days!

Study Your Competitors' "Hunting" Methodology!

The story below generated the market differentiator that netted us our largest client ever, and with whom we still enjoy a strong friendship.

Somewhere in the middle of 1999, my competitor study kept taking me back to one particular vendor of loose diamonds that was consistently beating me at the mat. It was a huge New York house, with a national and international reach, that had a massive inventory of fine goods. This diamond company had more people in its mailing room than I had in my entire organization (In 1999, my organization consisted of me and my wife.) Its "on hand" inventory back then was estimated at $400 million, and it had more money where that came from. It also had more loose diamonds on that month's "lost in inventory" list than I had in my vault. So, what and who cares? I had at least one "diamond," my health, thank G-d; I also had my Mazda 626, now with 200,000 miles on the clock, and clients that were active in the jewelry business. What else did I need, and why could I not get a chance to play with these clients that so regularly dealt with my competitor? Now, here's the thing: This company had already been in existence for three generations when I came to the United States. So, I had no problem understanding that fifty years of relationship, market presence and service history can somewhat establish an entity and ensure it a certain market share. This I could live with, but, I did not understand why I was not even being given a chance -- not even a window of opportunity to produce for an account! I was willing to trust customers with my merchandise; why were they not jumping at the chance to try me and my service? It wasn't that prospects were slamming doors on me -- that they had done the two years before. By now, I was sufficiently familiar to them to get in the door and to receive the "smile-thank you" treatment. Of course, you know what that is (you have experienced it hundreds of time); it is the response from a client prospect that is scripted at "buyers' school," and that is required course work in order to graduate; it is that ubiquitous "...uh-huh... uh-uh...smile...uh-huh...uh-huh...smile...uh-huh...well, thank you for coming in..." But, why was I not getting a crack at their business? What was the hold that this particular vendor had on its clients that did not allow for client entry from other vendors?

What made the situation even more frustrating for me was the fact that this particular vendor did not even have an area representative or salesman that serviced the western Pennsylvania market. All their business, with what should have been **my** clients, was being done by someone in the company's home office in New York, whom these clients had never met. I was hearing this vendor's name just too often to ignore and from potential accounts that were just too substantial. I had to do something. Well, what would that masterful solo hunter, the leopard, do?

I had clearly identified my true competitor; now, I needed to fully and completely research its "hunting" methodology and "closing" strategies. After using every tool available to me to do so, I began to study this vendor, its organization and its market offering. Google was not what it is today, and websites, back then, were still being developed and were entirely optional. Through my wife and her American accent, we made contact with this company, expressing interest in opening an account as a wholesale dealer, which I indeed intended to do – even competitors occasionally have a need to do business together. We gave them a P.O. Box mailing address and asked them to send us an entire company package and any other marketing material they had. They gladly did so, and, in typical large corporate fashion, that was the last we heard from them. We received their material and worked it over. My wife and I poured through it, made notes, and, a week or so later, held our first "Competitor Appreciation Day." The company was a monster -- in the kindest sense of the word – with massive financial, human, infrastructural and inventory resources! We clearly got that, gained some marketing ideas, learned some more industry terms, and, most of all, discovered how underfunded we really were. However, I was on the ground, in front of clients -- and local, offering the kind of service that it was simply impossible to duplicate from 400 miles away. We discussed this and revisited all the information and materials we had gathered on our competitor. My wife said to me, "Kivi, what leopard studies its competitor from a pamphlet and brochure?" I looked at her and said, "I got you!" Two weeks later, I had planned a trip to New York and had even invested in an airline ticket this time, although that is no guarantee against choking on cheap men's cologne! I had called up an internal salesman within the company and had said the following: "Hi there, my name is Kivi Bernhard. I am from South Africa, and I am in the diamond business. I will be in New York on a business trip and would love to meet your company." (All of this was, of course, true.) Seeing me as a prospective buyer that had "hunted" his company, he welcomed me in, confirming that he looked forward to receiving me at their New York headquarters at 3:00 pm.

I had arrived in the city at about eleven in the morning and had plenty of time to connect with some other New York contacts. Everywhere I went, I asked friends and colleagues about this vendor, gleaning as much information and "hunting" methodology as I could about the company, its employees and its owners. I went into the building that housed their operation; a floor above them, a floor below them, down the hall, across the hall. I walked around their block, studying the building itself, its other tenants, the street, its retailers, stores and businesses. Sounds criminal, right?

I arrived at my appointment promptly at three minutes past three o'clock, so as not to seem too eager. After five minutes of prime opportunity to study their reception area, the internal salesman greeted me, also not wanting to seem eager. We went into a meeting room attached to the reception area and commenced the standard exchanges of introduction and industry dialog. After a short time, I indicated that my primary objective was just to meet in person, see the office and establish a relationship. In response, the salesman said, "Well, let me just take you inside and show you around, and, when you get home, if there is anything you need, give me a call..." "Are you kidding?" I thought to myself. This was like winning the Lucky Leopard Lottery to study your "competitor predator." I commented that this would be great, and off we went. He took me right through the entire operation; I got right inside the bosom of my biggest competitor. I got a fleeting, but invaluable chance to see it all; their diamond traders' room, their marketing office, their vault room, their lunch room, the feel and culture of their office environment, etc. My eyes were just taking it all in and placing it on my memory hard drive for recall at a later time. This was prime Leopardology™ at work!

So, here it is! That day, having observed my competitor's entire operation, I attained and internalized a lot of "stuff" that offered me useful teaching points, information and intelligence. However, there was one small little thing I saw for, perhaps, two seconds, at most, that would develop into a game changer for my wholesale loose diamond business. The opportunity was hidden, not in any of the grandeur, opulence or technology. It was written on an A4 sheet of white bond paper with black ink and was taped to a door underneath a sign that identified that office as "Shipping & Mailing." The message simply read: "Attention all diamond traders – the cutoff for next day delivery diamond shipments is now 4:00 pm." At the bottom right hand corner of the paper there was a hand written addition in red pen that read – "No exceptions."

It hit me as I sat down in my window seat on the plane that would take me back to Pittsburgh, where we were living at the time. As I was looking out the window, observing the airport ground operations, I could see the small fleet of FedEx aircraft. That is what triggered the thought and brought the idea full circle. I landed in Pittsburgh at about 10:30 pm. As soon as I got off the plane and into the terminal, I immediately asked someone if, by any chance, FedEx had a shipping center at the Pittsburgh International Airport, and, if so, would he know where it was located; the answer was "yes" to both questions. I headed over there to find it closed. However, there was a sign that communicated to me that there was an airport handling center located on the airport service road, and that it closed at 11:30 pm. I made my way to the extended parking area, got into my car and proceeded directly to FedEx at the airport. Although it was 10:50 pm and dark, I did the "leopard thing" and attempted to acquaint myself with the area and the facility as best I could. I pulled up and went inside. I interviewed the assistant for information and received exactly what I needed.

I got home to my wife and my sleeping children at about 11:30 pm. My ever supportive wife greeted me with her effervescent smile and personality, which always makes me feel so blessed to have her in my life. We made our way to the couch into which I collapsed as I began downloading about my trip. She could hear the excitement in my voice, which sounded like I had just come back from a ten day business trip to Hong Kong and had signed the exclusive marketing rights to Coca-Cola! But, I hadn't. I had, however, defined an exclusive market offering and opportunity for our business from studying my competitor.

I sat up and energetically said to my wife, "I got it, Honey, and it's going to work for us!" I continued to articulate what I had learned by, firstly, identifying my true competitor, and, then, meticulously studying their hunting methodology. This is what I said:

I learned that their shipping department in New York closes at 4:00 pm sharp. If a client calls after 4:00 pm, they can still get through to a diamond trader, who can quote them on pricing and merchandise. However, they cannot get next day shipping service and have that diamond in their store for a next day morning delivery. Guess what, Sweetheart? We now have extended shipping hours! I checked it out while I was at the airport; FedEx has a center at the airport that receives next day delivery packages up until 11:00 pm. Tomorrow, we are going to launch a huge campaign and news release to all our clients stating that we now have extended shipping hours. We will announce that, in an attempt to offer a service of excellence to our valued clients, we have made specific arrangements with our shippers (a three minute discussion with FedEx at the airport to enquire into their hours) and our internal shipping department (my wife and me) to extend our shipping hours. We will announce, effective immediately, that we are excited to present our clients an exclusive market offering of next-day delivery guarantee for orders placed before 9:30 pm EST.

My wife looked at me and said, "Done…great idea…let's make it happen!" And, so we did. That's exactly what we did – we announced it with as much enthusiasm and professionalism as we could afford. This campaign was our new "baby," and we blasted it to our client base using every possible method of delivery. With as much of a splash as we could create, we plastered our campaign slogan **"Call Me Later!"** with our toll free number and extended shipping hours wherever we could. Every memorandum, invoice, statement and communication from us now delivered the news with a sticker or a bright red insert. We kept the campaign alive, not for a month or so, but for a solid year. It was received with much interest, along with that other required verbal response they teach you at "buyers' school:" "That's good to know -- we will keep that in mind." You, of course, are listening to this response thinking, "Great! -- another thing that this guy without a mind is going to keep in it!" But, hey – welcome to the world of business development. The fact was, however, that I knew that our campaign was trickling its way in and getting attention from owners and buyers. Although the result was not immediate, most noticeably I could sense that it had registered with my clients as a significant market offering that really filled a need. It might have been a need that they did not currently have, but they took note of it, knowing that it would be a need that would arise -- just a question of when. Specifically, I began to target my telephone marketing to two client groups: firstly, clients that regularly used my New York competitor; secondly, clients of this vendor on the west coast, operating in a different time zone, who were having to place orders with this vendor as early as 1:00 pm. I would call stores between four and five in the afternoon, knowing that the New York vendor, in particular, was closed for shipping. I would simply ask if there was anything that they, perhaps, needed for the next day. Certainly, you understand, that for weeks on end, I would hear "No thanks, we are all set." (PS: That's another thing they teach at "buyers' school.") But, that was OK, because I knew that, every time I reinforced this clearly defined market differentiator to my client, I was providing a solution to a need that was inevitably due to arise. When that time came and that need arose, I knew that, due to weeks, months or even years of communication of that solution, we were uniquely in line to receive that business. I would sometimes stay on those phones as late as 9:00 pm EST, working the west coast, late night independents and mall stores. I was all about our extended shipping hours and unique brand of personalized service. And, when that "Yes, we do!" reply came through the wires every once in a while, I was on it like a fly on dung (a South African bush expression). I would pull that diamond out of the vault, prepare the paper work, get everything into a FedEx shipping box, get me and the box into my 1987 Mazda 626 and make the 50 minute round trip to the FedEx handling center at the Pittsburgh International Airport. Guess what! Next day by 10:30 am, my client had a stone in his hand for presentation to his customer. I had serviced a client, and he could, in turn, service his.

It worked, and, with G-d's help, became a significant aspect of our business. Due to our perseverance and belief in this strategy's ability to get me in play with clients, it began to happen. After several weeks, or even months, we began to receive calls that sounded something like this:

"Hi there...we are looking for…and New York was closed for shipping, so we thought we would give you a try..." It was music to my ears and allowed me to service a client and begin building a performance history with him. In short order, I began to get "daytime" calls and to become a preferred vendor with many of these accounts. We became known as the company that was open "late" or that had "extended shipping hours," and I share with you that, to this very day, we are still known as such. We have many clients and friends that we closed and brought on board through this campaign, including our largest volume client.

We did this by studying our "competitor predator." It, in turn, defined our specific client opportunity and market differentiator.

If It Works For Your Competition... It Should Not Work For You!

Ok, so we grew up learning that what is good for the goose is good for the gander! Well, guess what, they are "married" to each other. Follow me here, please – you are not "married" to your competitor! If something is working well for one of your competitors in the market place, by definition it is not suitable for you. Well, it is, if you and your corporation want to be known as a "copy-cat serial seller." However, if you seek to truly gain market penetration and branding, you are going to have to be an originator, creator and proprietor of fresh market offerings -- an initiator of ideas, not a duplicator. The market place is flooded. We have more supply of most commodities on earth than we do demand. This obviously may not be accurate with regards certain natural resources, but this certainly is the case with most services, professions and produced or manufactured commodities. So, if, for example, you produce Boeing jets, or Maserati luxury sports cars, you get to enjoy a 12 to18 month waiting list, which definitely creates more demand than supply. However, on closer investigation, you will learn that this demand is engineered and fabricated. You do realize, of course, that Boeing or Maserati could easily open another plant to handle the backlog, but there is not sufficient **demand** to warrant that. And so, at the risk of being challenged by micro and macro economists alike, I humbly submit that, by and large, our consumer markets are simply oversupplied. Therefore, when we entrepreneurs and business people make an offering in the market place, we absolutely have to do so from a place of innovation, creativity and originality. The chances are that your service or product already exists somewhere in our consolidated global economy. What does not exist, yet, is your specific market offering -- the innovative, original and creative edge of your market offering that separates you from the "pack" of similar services and products that are already available to your prospective clients. Unless you are an inventor of new products, science or technology, it is extremely unlikely that what you are offering to the market place is not already in the market place. Incidentally, with the speed and reach of the internet today, even if you have just invented something brand new (the flushing toilet or light bulb, for example), the chances are that a similar, but slightly different, version will appear on the market within six to eight weeks. It's called -- China. Oh, and new service offerings that arise from evolving market conditions, like "social media coach" or "how to get your share of government TARP money coach," are duplicated within hours. Well, how long does it take to put up a website? -- Ok, 24 hours for a really sharp website that allows the public to think you have been at this for years. That's how long it takes.

So, now that I have totally depressed you and deflated your entrepreneurial spirit no end, please allow me to share with you that what I just shared with you above was the good news!

Absolutely, it's good news! Imagine, if, at your beck and call, you had 24 hours a day, 7 days a week, 365 days a year access to a high level information source that could guide and direct you towards your market differentiator -- something that could give you market research and estimated results before you even launched your business offering – something that could provide you with a precise, honest, subjective and independent opinion as to exactly just how innovative, creative and original your market offering really is – something that could offer you unhindered access to key nuances and details that would, in fact, define your specific market opportunity – something that could supply you with the very information that would shape the destination of your business, that would allow for its market penetration, and that would allow it to actually rise above the noise of the alternative offerings that are out there! This would be huge! I mean, wouldn't it be incredible to have something or someone whose sole purpose would be to highlight and underscore your particular market differentiator, which, as we have established, is exactly the thing that clients and customers are buying – something or someone to continually be your "differentiator watch dog," ensuring that you are innovating and not just duplicating - an entity that would dedicate its entire infrastructure and all of its resources to doing nothing but guiding you and your organization towards your competitive edge and towards the thing that distinguishes you from others. This would be really huge! Just imagine if you had all this, literally, at your fingertips!

Well you do! -- It's called a **competitor**.

Chapter 8

My Zebra Wears "Prada"!

Positive Predatory Pillar ™ No. 4

In the bush:

Study Your Prey: Leopard will spend 25% of their waking hours simply observing, studying and noting the movements and behavior of their prey.

Listen and respond to your client's needs, not yours.

I REMEMBER IT so clearly: It was 1992 in the middle of the South African summer heat of December, in a severe drought that was now in its third year. I was deep in the bush near the northeast region of Polokwane. You have no idea how hot and dry it was! We had seen cheetah earlier in the day, thin and exhausted due to the scarcity of "client opportunities" that had resulted from the lack of water. Lukas, my tracker, spotted the leopard way before I did. It was 2:15 pm -- the middle of the day -- precisely the wrong time to see leopard. They are mostly nocturnal and remain very secluded during the day, not wanting to give up their cover. But, there it was, in more than broad daylight, this beautiful large female following a dry river bed. I mean very dry! After getting over the excitement of seeing my leopard in the bush, I exclaimed to my tracker, "Wow, what is she doing near a dry river bed, out there, taking a risk being so exposed, and with zero chance of a successful hunt?" My tracker, a fifth generation Shongaan-Zulu born to the bush, looked at me and said, "Fool, she is preparing for her hunt when the river **will** flow again!" I immediately understood what he had said, and, at that moment, received a lifelong lesson in change management and market endurance.

In an effort to dramatically increase their "close rate" by clearly defining their "client approach" strategy, leopard will spend hours a day, and some at night, merely studying the movements and habits of various prey. On occasion, leopard have been known to even forgo what seems like an apparent hunt opportunity, so as not to disturb the chance to study prey in a particular situation. It is a remarkable discipline to observe. They have a clear and unequivocal commitment to holding back now in exchange for being that much more effective later. Wow, what a concept! – but, a really tough sell in a world and society that wants what it wants -- and wants it now! Of course, however, the rewards need no introduction or explanation. As we are learning throughout this book, there is a reason why leopard close a whopping 76% of all "client closure" attempts; this is one of them. Studying their prey with the same meticulous attention that is paid to studying their territory affords them invaluable information that will guide their "client approach" and "client closure" strategy.

It was just Howard and me. My wife had gifted me a five day bush trip with my old buddy, doing what we love to do -- getting surrounded and swallowed by Africa and its wildlife. Ok, so we did have a bottle of 12 year old Glenfiddich and some Cohiban cigars with us, but, beyond that, we were deep in G-d's country. Life was good! There were blue skies and glorious winter sun, and the weather was temperate, or so we thought, based on the day we got into the bush. Mid-afternoon on our second day, the skies opened with a downpour that would last the next two days. It wasn't cold during the day, but it was seriously wet; small drinking pools and river tributaries were beginning to flood, soaking the sand banks and bush land around them. It was just wet, dirty and uncomfortable to be out in the bush, looking for game viewing opportunities – you got to love it! While we had a brand new 4x4 rental land rover, fully equipped with "stuck in the mud" stuff, visibility was low, and we obviously had to be particularly alert and aware of our surroundings. In those conditions, the bigger concern comes from getting stuck in the home territory of buffalo and elephant. In heavy rain, they tend to come together in large numbers in an attempt to offer shelter and body heat to each other. It is also a very vulnerable time for them, and for their young in particular. Their normal defense mechanisms of sight, sound and smell are heavily compromised by the rain, and their predators know this. Buffalo, especially, are very edgy in these conditions and can become very aggressive. African buffalo, at the best of times, are very dangerous and are potentially lethal. Believe it or not, even with their large size, they are not that easy to see, and, often, you will suddenly find yourself a little too close for comfort. It was about 10:00 am, and we were sitting in a thatch hide that was desperately doing all it could to keep us dry, as we watched the rain thunder down, another day of potential game viewing vanishing. Or, so we thought! While we were in the hide, I had shared with Howard something my tracker friend Lukas had taught me: In the bush lands and savannahs of Africa, immediately after heavy rains have fallen, there is a time of debriefing and regrouping for all the inhabitants; birds need to assess damage to nests, honey badgers must evaluate mud holes, hyena need to check dens, crocodile must inspect river banks, etc. Things in the environment will have shifted, and new or different conditions now prevail. Forget about "Who moved my cheese?" It is more like, "G-d just moved my entire world as I knew it." Even after a short but heavy rainstorm, perhaps accompanied by one of those spectacular lightning shows that makes New Year's fireworks in Las Vegas look amateurish, it is possible that, for the wildlife, the world as they knew it has changed. Parenthetically, imagine experiencing the "day after" effect of something like the Bear Sterns and Lehman Brothers collapse several times a month -- or several times a day in some seasons. It takes a certain change management agility and leadership skill to deal with this on such a regular and consistent basis. It is possible for lightning or flooded rivers to change the entire ecology of a region in minutes, and so, while the generalities might be the same, the details have most likely changed. If you are a leopard, dependant on your knowledge of self and the environment around you for survival, it is exactly those details that may make the difference between life and death. You are now going to need to get out into your hunting territory again and re-familiarize yourself with your "market place," retaking inventory of things you knew and becoming acquainted with new things you previously did not know. Once again, leopard instinctively understand this to be an asset, not a liability. It is an opportunity to discover newly fallen trees and debris that will afford them cover and stealth. It is an opportunity to examine which grazing lands have been destroyed, and which have been opened to herds. It is an opportunity for leopard to re-invent themselves in their market place, building on previous successes, discarding old failures and refining better "client approach" strategies.

As if G-d had just turned the tap off, it suddenly let up. We were now left with the considerable dripping of large droplets coming off the treetops and tall brush of mopane thickets. There was that unmistakable scent of, "I have just watered my African Garden of Eden – signed: G-d" that is robust with all sorts of messaging to the trained nose. The cloud cover was still thick, but the intermittent rainbow, coming from an easterly direction, was calling to its partner the sun to peak through and introduce itself. It was as if the Grand Maestro, Himself, had stepped into nature's orchestra pit and summoned anything and everything possessing an instrument of any sort. With bird life in the lead, all together at once, G-d's creatures struck up an opus that would have made Beethoven hear again. The earth was soaked, dry had become wet, wet had become flowing, and flowing is another word for "life" in Africa. Everyone had gotten the memo about the rain having stopped, and heads and ears began appearing out of crevices and holes we never knew existed. Kudu (large African antelope) came out of nowhere to enjoy a medley of rainwater and mopane leaves. A spectacular malachite kingfisher, having just received the full service option from nature's version of a car wash, landed on the soaked branch of a knob thorn tree. An uncommon sighting of a long-tailed paradise whydah bird was, itself, a breathtaking view. But, the true gift of "rare game sighting" that we were blessed to view was a pair of sable antelope. These majestic and regal animals are known as the royalty amongst Africa's antelope, and, because of their scarcity, are very rare to see. They are a sight to behold! Exquisitely painted in deep black and tones of grey, with an underbelly and face of snow white, and with streaks of red and orange, sable antelope boast a formidable pair of horns that curl back to a sharp point and can grow as long as three feet. They are a distinctive and privileged game viewing opportunity for which one is eternally grateful to his Creator. These two antelope were evidently nearby and simply appeared about fifty feet in front of us, moving away from the direction of a now boisterous river. Howard and I made our way to our 4x4, which now needed every bit of its abilities to keep us rolling. The water had eroded parts of the sand roads, leaving deep crevasses filled with mud and water; there was a lot of pooling in some areas of the road, and the sides of the road were now water streams with bush grass on one side and thick grab mud walls on the other. It was fun, but not that clever, to be out in those conditions. That African mud can truly hold you and your 4x4, and you will get nowhere fast. We were trying to make our way back to camp to get some breakfast and some sleep after our morning long expedition, which had begun at 5:30 am. The air was crisp and fresh and had that healthy taste to it that holds the promise of "good stuff" ahead. Howard turned to me, while I was fighting with the clutch, and said: "We will see leopard before we get back to camp." You have no idea how I wish he had been talking about the state lottery! It was not five minutes later that we came to the top of a rise in the road. About 20 feet in, we saw a family of about nine warthogs busily assessing and repairing some damage to their mud mounds and burrows. We could see the alpha male on the perimeter, nervously standing watch while his wife consulted the "interior decorators" and project managed the busy family. The rains had clearly created change in their lives, and they were now occupied with managing it. I stopped the land rover and took in the sight for a few moments. I took a pair of binoculars and scanned my left and right to catch what my unaided eyes did not. I did! It was huge and commanded respect. You just knew that this female leopard was a seasoned and experienced hunter with years of "market" and "client" study behind her.

She was standing perfectly still with her head and body trained in the direction of the warthogs. This was "predatory freeze," and everything she had was summoned to be entirely present for this occasion. Her ears were pointed forward, her nostrils fully open, her eyes fixed on her subject matter, which was north of her position. She was invisible to the warthogs, because she was upwind and could not be seen in the tall grass and grey cloud cover that came to her aid. She kept her neck line level with the top of the grass line, never taking her eyes off the warthog, not even to look at us. Her ears took care of that, rotating back in our direction every so often. It was about 20 seconds since we had spotted her, and she had not moved. We both thought, "This is it! I mean this is the big one you spend years visiting the bush and hoping to see -- sometime -- a daytime, unhindered view of a leopard hunt from "prospecting" to "client closure." This was going to be the hunt we had "hunted" for years. We said nothing; we were so freaking hyped! I took the binoculars up again and took a good look. I said to Howard, No, buddy...it's not going happen." After barraging me with an eloquently strung sequence of light profanities in four different languages,(a particular talent of his), Howard asked, "Why not?" "Her tail is curled and flickering white! She is just **studying** these warthogs, Howard - - she is not hunting them," I said, in a disappointed whisper, though not dismissing what we were seeing.

I explained that the under part of the end of a leopard's tail is white. All feline predators, but leopard, specifically, use their tails to communicate information, and even the smallest of nuances, to co-hunters and to their young. Lukas once taught me that leopard will actually use the white of their tail to communicate to potential prey, and to others that might blow their cover, that they are **not** in hunt mode -- quite literally, waving a white peace flag. This incredible, instinctive, natural genius allows leopard to get right up close to observe, watch and study potential "clients" and their behavior. It is ingenious, because, by so doing, they will pick up all sorts of "client" intelligence that can later be used to carve out and define a successful "client approach." Information, the significant and the insignificant, can all come together to enhance their "close rate" and minimize risk when they are hunting. Tremendously valuable "client" details that were previously gathered can now exponentially increase their potential for success by defining a "client entry" and "closing" strategy.

Beyond teaching us the invaluable lesson that closing a client is not a one-size-fits-all proposition, leopard have offered us tremendous insight into a fundamental truth of "client closure." Leopard do not want to be where their prey is. They will be seen, thereby decreasing their chance of closure and increasing the risk of the hunt. They want to be where their prey is not -- but will be! Leopard use the element of surprise, initiating the hunt rather than responding to it. This is big and a substantial insight into "client closure" technique. You see, by studying their prey and its behavior, leopard are able to establish what is the most primordial of all behavior – habit -- what their prey **always** does! Examples of this would include: what water source they always use; what path they always take to get there; where they always stop to graze or rest on the way; who always stands watch and where; who always pays attention, and who never does; what hole a particular warthog always uses to enter or exit its burrow; what pair of impala are always together; what "designer clothing" a particular Zebra always wears, etc. Habitual behavior will allow leopard to be exactly where their "client" is not, but will be soon. They know, based on hours of accumulative "client" study and the guarantee of "habit forming behavior," that, while their "client" opportunity is not yet in sight, it absolutely will be. Their function is to position themselves to be in the right place at the right time. This is possible through a commitment to studying their "client."

We are all creatures of habit, are we not? We all frequent the same coffee shop we always go to, play tennis on the same courts we always play on, fish on the same lake we always fish on, eat in the same restaurants we always eat in, go to the same movie theatres we always go to, use the same gas station we always use, and buy the same flavor ice cream we always buy. The association meeting we always attend, or the one we never do, rarely changes; the paper we always read, or never do, rarely changes.

If you are my client prospect, and I am initiating a closure opportunity with you, my function is to be where you are not, but will be soon. It may take me weeks, months or years to get an appointment with you at your office. However, it will take me a little bit of client study and research to "coincidentally" bump into you at the coffee house you use every morning. And, by the way, the $20.00 donation that my wife and I made to the American Heart Association in your name – yeah, that was after I "googled" your name and learned that you sit on the board of the local chapter. What wonderful work you do...

Predatory Prey Profiling...Politically Incorrect!

Not to be repetitive, but let's look at this again. Clients are not a one-size-fits-all proposition. We say this, and we say it often, but we don't always mean it; we, therefore, jeopardize our success rate and closure rate while on the "hunt." The temptation to do business often overrides and clouds our ability to think clearly about what really is "closable" and what is not!

Leopard have an instinctive awareness of this component of their survival. They clearly and continually assess "client" prospects, not only for their feasibility with regards return-on-investment, but with regards the viability of the "deal" at all: In other words, can I close this "client?" There is an instinctive and careful assessment that quickly takes place in order to facilitate this process. It is an immediate "prey profiling" that happens in an instant and then receives confirmation based on further information. Leopard need to establish the following in a matter of seconds: Am I equipped, without having to go outside of my own tooling and resources, with what is needed to close this client?; Is it a feasible, nutritious "client" that I will be able to hold in a tree, post closure?; And, does the gain outweigh the risk involved in closing this particular client? The answer to these "prey profiling" questions are "yes" or "no," and the law of the jungle does not leave any room for a "maybe." Nor does the "jungle" of commerce!

Prey selection is such an integral component of leopard behavior that it features as a major and unique part of their "school syllabus" when they are young. There is an unusual anomaly with leopard that we do not find with lion or cheetah. Lion cubs and sub-adults learn how to hunt by accompanying the pride on the hunt. They will be positioned at the back of the pride in sight of their mothers' ears and tails, both of which have distinctive markings that will transmit teaching information to the youngsters. Survival on the plains of the African savannah is really about only two things – "hunting" and "killing." (Before you say "Ooooh!" please note that it is no different where you and I live; it's just called "prospecting" and "closing.") And, so it is. If you can successfully do both these things, and do them well, you stand a chance in the African bush lands. It is no wonder, therefore, that these two qualities are instinctive to most predators, including lion cubs. By observing the adults hunt and kill, and by attempting to do the same, cubs and sub-adults finesse their skill level and ability to "close deals." However, it is interesting that leopard cubs seem to instinctively know to hunt for food, but not to kill it. Only after trial and error, after realizing that, if they do not "sign and seal" the deal, it will get away from them, do young leopard learn to kill. This is unusual and also counterintuitive for one of the most precise and efficient "killing machines" on earth. One would expect the exact opposite to be the case. But, it is not, and for a very fascinating and informative reason -- to teach them the skill and benefit of "client selection."

Because leopard cubs have to learn for themselves exactly how to kill their prey, it continually reinforces exactly what their killing ability is and gives them a precise knowledge of what they can close, and what they cannot close! In other words, it turns out that, in the wild, "killing" is not one-size-fits-all either. While one may be equipped with the tooling necessary to "close" a banded mongoose, for example, it does not mean that one has what it takes to "close" a steenbok (very small antelope). As young leopard discover their "killing" ability, how it works, when it works and on what it works, they incidentally discover their ideal prey profile. They get a critical sense of what exactly their "closing" apparatus and ability is, which in turn defines their perfect "client profile." Additionally, this process of having to learn, firstly, to "close clients," and, secondly, **how** to "close clients" has a secondary affect that is tremendous; it builds a visceral confidence for what will become instinctive within them. I am referring to "killing," because this is something they have to "learn" to do; they get the opportunity to actually take ownership of it, so to speak -- they learn that this is something they can do, and that they can do well. They have watched it develop and grow within them, and they have observed the various stages of its success. At the back end, they become independent territorial adults that have graduated from the "school of killing prey," as opposed to "I was born this way." This could well explain what is responsible for their abundant confidence and exactness with regards "closing." Leopard take no prisoners! They do not seem to have a neutral gear; it seems to be either "drive" or "reverse." Once they select their "client," it is "closed"; it just does not know it yet. This is emphasized by the precision and intensity of the throat-clutch strategy leopard use to "sign" the "closing paperwork" -- nature's version of a Mont Blanc pen deal signing.

But this confidence of self and acute awareness of its ability to kill does not manifest in cockiness, giving it mandate to "transact" anywhere and everywhere it pleases. Quite the contrary! It seems to make leopard much more disciplined hunters, finely attuned to what is within their "selling" ability, and what is not. They instinctively will decline large takes and what appear to the human eye to be "extremely profitable" hunt opportunities, knowing that it is out of reach for them to successfully "close." An African buffalo, for instance, offers 2,500 pounds of profit -- if you are a lion pride with 13 members contributing huge "corporate and conglomerate resources" to this "client project." But, certainly not, if you are a solo, solitary hunter, dependant on the finesse and "closing" precision of your extremely effective but smaller "organization." This instinctive attribute that leopard have, the ability to say "thank you, but no thank you" and "these teeth are not for everyone," not only keeps them alive, but it also maintains their extraordinarily high close rate and success. While not, perhaps, socially or even politically correct, declining certain client opportunities will not only prevent you from doing bad business, it will also keep you in business. (Ask the small community banks that **did not** get into the domestic mortgage business.)

Hey, what do you know? – Prey opportunities in the African bush are much like clients in the jungle of commerce; they are specific to the "closing" ability of the "prospector."

"The success of your hunt is directly proportionate to your ability to kill it…do not hunt what you cannot kill."

Taken from 7 Habits of Highly Effective Leopard; Author: G-d

Why Leopard Don't Use LinkedIn (or Twitter).

John Varty, the world renowned wildlife photographer, conservationist, big cat expert and family proprietor of the great, (and famous for its leopard), Londolozi Private Game Reserve in South Africa, once shared the following with me. It is well-known that, when the opportunity presents itself, feline predators will rob a "client" from another predator. However, when that does occur, leopard, and many other predators, will be selective about the freshness of the kill. In general, predators prefer freshly killed meat that they, themselves, have "closed" but will not hesitate to steal a competitor's fresh kill.

The theory behind this moves beyond the desire for fresh, nutritious meat that offers maximum return-on-investment for the energy and risk taken to get it. Beyond that, there is an intrinsic and instinctive need feline predators have to "transact" with their "clients," first hand. This is a fundamental element of good relationship development and a core component of Leopardology™.

Understanding that nothing at all can replace front line "client" time, leopard will rarely scavenge prey from other hunters. Not being intrinsically involved in the "transactional" part of a "client relationship" will rob them of major opportunities to fully grasp "client" nuances and behaviors. As they are "closing" their prey, leopard will have a substantial learning rendezvous with that prey. It is a most valued chance to really "feel" and "touch" the essence of what makes their client tick -- literally! Follow me here; if you are a leopard, and success for you means effective killing of prey, wouldn't you want every close-up chance you could get to find out what really keeps your prey alive? Handling the "closure" of their prey, first hand, offers leopard exactly this -- a regular and consistent opportunity to have first hand confirmation of previously gathered "client" study information and to discover new data. Hunting territory conditions change, and so does the makeup and constitution of its inhabitants. The availability of water, as well as the absence or presence of various grasses, brush, thickets, fauna and flora, can dramatically impact the well-being of antelope and "client" options. Getting your "paws" on your "client" and really sinking your teeth into the "client contact" is, quite literally, an opportunity to take the "pulse" of the market – in the real sense of the word. As a leopard, it gives you current and accurate information with regards "client" health. Just how healthy and strong are they? Just how agile and alert are they? Exactly how strong are their necks, and how thick are those windpipes? What is the current need that the "market" is not supplying them, which may drive them elsewhere? This commitment to a "paws on" approach in handling their client truly allows them to identify "client" proficiencies, as well as deficiencies, in a way that "textbook" study or "long distance learning" simply cannot. This could well be a contributor to their exceptionally high "close rate" -- irrespective of the hunting territory they find themselves in.

All too often, we back away from, or delegate to others, perhaps the most valuable and critical part of client interaction -- face time and closing! There is no more precise laboratory of exploration for client need and behavior than the eyeball to eyeball signing and handshake at the time of transaction. It is often worth more than the deal itself. For, within it lies the messaging and client approach for the repeat and future business to be done.

In general, our society has committed itself, under the guise of technological "growth," to removing the human experience from the business, and, in fact, from the entire social equation. It has become perfectly acceptable to transact with people, and even marry them, using social media on the internet -- an entirely impersonal and anonymous exchange that only affords its participants a result, and nothing more. We have promoted its use under the banner of **speed** and **convenience** -- two idols of the 21st century. We are convinced that the quicker we can do something, and the more convenient it is, the more viable and feasible it is. I humbly submit to my readers that, in our ferocious attempt to satiate this addictive appetite of my fellow GenX peers and the Y'ers behind them, we have removed a staple of effective and stable interaction. Personal human connection is becoming a lost art, and, I would submit, is eroding "client" relationships. In doing some research for this book, I was informed by the Department of Commerce that this current generation has made more money than the last six generations before it combined. (I can only assume the same applies to the money we have recently lost in the market.)

So, while technology has contributed to exponential growth in terms of the quantity of transacting we have been doing, I suggest that it has dramatically reduced the quality of it. We have simply made and lost more money than previous generations. Could it be that previous generations, in fact, had to do less work than we do, and for better business (maybe not as much of it, but better qualitatively)? It occurred to me that, with all the communication technology we have at our disposal today, previous generations had a key element that we, by and large, do not -- client relationships! Regular, in-person client contact and the notion of being there for the "close," when plausible, ensured special and qualitative friendships and business relationships. Yeah, it was not as easy as the click of a button, and it did not happen instantaneously. But, somehow, it stuck better and created better quality business, infused with more of the values that the human experience offers.

Take a look at the sheer volume and magnitude of business that has just come unglued since November of 2008. So much of it is riddled with suggestions of impropriety and dishonesty -- a lack of integrity, trust, faith and reliance. How were so many and such a large volume of transactions void of these tenets of basic business? The computer cannot message any of these human attributes. That's how!

No, I am not suggesting that there is no value to be had in the incredible power of the internet and social media networks. (Please check out my YouTube video.) I am, however, submitting that the likes of Plaxo, Twitter and LinkedIn are **tools** for "client" contact and communication. But, they are not a **replacement** for it!

Leopard will rarely, if ever, give up the golden opportunity to come into physical contact with their prey. It is an irreplaceable fact-finding opportunity that will greatly enhance their efficacy and success rate.

Cobra Venom Can Kill!

For most of Africa's predators, the snake, venomous or non-venomous, is a conundrum. On the one hand, it offers a nutritious and tempting meal. On the other hand, however, it can prove not only dangerous, but sometimes fatal. A very careful assessment of the return on investment and risk-to-reward ratio needs to be established when prospecting such a "client." The snake, in concept, is a relatively easy "close" that does not require the exertion of much energy and effort. It is also a profitable proposition with a great "meat to bone" ratio, convenient to handle and less cumbersome than an antelope, for example. However, if it is a venomous species or a large constrictor, it can kill you! Clearly, you see the dilemma here? A wet bite from an Egyptian cobra, puff adder or mamba can be fatal or cause a disabling injury that would prevent a predator from hunting in the future, which itself would prove fatal.

If the snake is not venomous, not only would this be an entirely safe "client" option, but a most viable hunt, too. But, often, in the bush, it is not so easy to know, even if you are a leopard and the African bush is your permanent residence. There are species that, initially, look similar to one another -- except for the fact that one will kill you while the other is entirely harmless. There are, for example, species of black mole snake that are entirely non-venomous, but which, at first glance, can appear almost identical to the infamous and fatal black mamba.

Often, lion, leopard and cheetah will come upon snakes inadvertently, startling themselves and the snake. For instance, there have been sightings of fully grown male lion that have become ill and have ultimately died from cobra bites that were incurred by accidentally stepping over a rock formation or grass covering, disturbing the snake. It is for this reason that, instinctively, predators simply stay away from snakes as viable "client" options. While there are snake specialists like the secretary bird, banded mongoose or honey badger, who have made detailed "client study" analysis of these snakes and are equipped with specific assets to "close" these clients, the rule of thumb is that leopard and other feline predators decline this particular "client engagement." Only trial and error, sometimes fatal, will give leopard the experience and skill necessary to take on this fairly abundant, but potentially lethal, prey. Outside of competitor predators, venomous snakes are the next biggest obstacle for young cubs and sub-adults attempting to live to maturity.

What is fascinating to observe is how "market conditions" will influence leopard's and other predators' decision to hunt snakes and consider them for "client" opportunity. For instance, when drought conditions prevail and food sources lessen, snakes move way up on the menu, because they tend to stick around and are very territorial. The risk, of course, has not changed in any way, but, as other options diminish, their feasibility increases, and they get more and more consideration. Here is the teaching point of Leopardology™, that this offers: When market conditions change, a fascinating thing will happen; leopard will actively start revisiting their instinctive knowledge of snakes and will re-embark specifically on "snake study" opportunities. My trusted tracker and friend, Lukas, has told me that, when these conditions have occurred, he has seen leopard spend more time than usual cleaning and sharpening their drew claws. This is clearly about re-tooling for a specific "client closure" attempt. It is their claw, and the dexterity and speed of their paw and claw work, that is going to determine success in "closing" snakes! Successful snake hunts, while very dangerous for leopard, are, nonetheless, clearly within their scope and ability to "close." It is a stretch for them, but not outside their capability. However, it is, in general, a very occasional "client" for specific benefit and use.

Undoubtedly, hunting less familiar prey requires a refresher course and re-acquaintance with the prey, strategy, equipment and assets that are going to be used to hunt and kill it. Because of their unwavering commitment to studying their prey, when they have to consider snake as prey, and on the rare occasions that they do so, leopard "close" snake hunts more successfully than their competitors.

We all have clients that are high maintenance or even financially "dangerous" to close. In our current economic "drought," when market conditions are diminishing our options and forcing us to do business with some of these clients, we must do what that master hunter, the leopard, does. We must revisit and study these particular clients and their inherent trading danger, identifying and anticipating it. Our opportunity, then, is to revisit what assets, tooling and resources we have within our organization to offset or neutralize the potential risk of doing this business; one must mobilize these assets and re-acquaint oneself with them and how they are used. For example: An escrow account that your company has may well have been lying dormant. Reactivating it now in order to receive a deposit from this potentially risky client, in advance of a shipment, is your equivalent of a leopard sharpening its claws before it attempts to hunt a venomous snake.

The tough global market is moving us to look at accounts and clients, which we would otherwise forego. While potentially viable and within your selling ability, it is possible that these particular clients might "kill" you. Now, more than ever -- **Study Your "Prey"!**

Chapter 9

Clients Are Like A Book... Read Them!

Positive Predatory Pillar ™ No. 4

In the boardroom:

Study Your Prey: Leopard will spend 25% of their waking hours simply observing, studying and noting the movements and behavior of their prey.

Listen and respond to your client's needs, not yours.

TAKE A LOOK at how ridiculous this is. We spend most of our business lives looking anywhere and everywhere we can for the answers to client and profit conundrums. The assumption is that the answer is always out there; it is with a consultant we need to hire, or a marketing firm we need to contract, or an organizational development team we need to employ. It is clearly about getting your hands on something that you do not already have; a DVD training series, a CD audio series, or a book you need to buy. (P.S. Please buy my book.) Seldom do we truly consider the real solution to be found in something we already possess -- something already acquired and gained that is on tap and available to offer answers at any time and at no further cost. Some of the most precise and beneficial advice and strategic planning that money can buy is available to you through something that you already have in house. Your client!

It was a Thursday, mid-morning in February of 2000, when we were still living in Pittsburgh. Need I say more? Sheets of wet, slushy snow were falling, making the roads treacherous, while offering what

I came to call, "funeral home décor." You got it! -- that awful, dark, dreary, dingy, gray backdrop that ages everything around you by one hundred years. By the way, in Pittsburgh, Pennsylvania, that can get serious, because the most recently constructed thing around is, in fact, likely to be the local funeral home, probably now in its fourth generation- - OK, so maybe only in its third generation! But, you get the point here -- cold and crappy, and descriptive of my thoughts on the many occasions I would look in the mirror and ask myself what the heck I had done by leaving sunny South Africa; what had I done by leaving my family, my friends, my business network and my bush! (I discovered that doing this every so often was much cheaper than seeing a shrink or taking some of that Prozac.) After pulling back from the mirror and snapping back into my reality, I could now get on with it and make something happen.

So, that particular day, I decided that I was going to "hunt" Marks Jewelers (not their real name) in Zelienople, Pennsylvania. Oh yeah – I am not making this up. Zelienople is about 45 miles north of Pittsburgh and is another famous spot on the map. It is home to a very upscale and established retail jeweler that services a focused group of old money, retirees and the residents of the town, most of whom are employed in various manufacturing operations. Zelienople is home to Zipelli, the famous fireworks vendors. But, beyond the two streets and the corners of Main Street and 1st Street, there is not much in the way of fireworks going on there; just my kind of town -- small pond, big fish. Now, I had been prospecting Marks Jewelers for some time, without much success. Yes, we had done some small test-the-waters business, but we had not transacted in the big leagues yet, and I was convinced that we needed to do so. Early on arriving in the USA, a friend of mine in Pittsburgh had sat me down one day and had given me the whole rundown regarding the Carnegie/Mellon industrial history of Pittsburgh. He had informed me that the subsequent generations were living in these small suburban spots with tons of "cash under the mattress" and disposable income. This not only gave me hope that there was significant business to be done in the region, but it also told me, or so I thought, precisely where this business was to be done. I had not physically been out to the Marks Jewelers location, and, on the occasions that Mark and I had met, it had been in Pittsburgh. In my mind, they were obviously servicing these "old money" third and fourth generation "industrial heirs," who now occupied the sprawling hills of towns just like Zelienople, Pennsylvania. All along, I had pegged Marks Jewelers as an ideal and exact "client profile" to do large stone business -- big, two, three and four carat diamonds for pendants, earrings and engagement rings, being paid for by Carnegie and Mellon money. I was sure that such business was being done -- just not by me. Marks Jewelers was an old, longstanding, highly reputable retail jeweler that had strong vendor relationships well in place. In fact, I knew who they were because of Positive Predatory Pillar No.3 – Study Your Competitor Predator.

I knew that all I had to do was get in -- get into the store, gain their trust and leave a tangible trail. I was totally convinced that there were significant diamonds flying out of that store every day, and the problem was simply that I was not supplying them. Confident that the difficulty I was experiencing was due to the fact that Marks Jewelers did not perceive me capable of supplying such merchandise, I came up with a plan of action. Clearly, while we had established some degree of trust and reliability based on the small business we had done, Marks Jewelers was unaware that, with my connections in South Africa, I had the inventory and capability to supply them significant, gem quality loose diamonds; I was able to do a lot more than just serve as a "local diamond dealer" with a wallet of "smalls." Evidently, they were not educated to this, and, without a doubt, they needed to be. Well, that Thursday was the day Marks Jewelers would receive this education. And so, I pulled out a map, worked the route to Zelienople, timed it out and prepared to leave my office -- however, not before taking care of an important detail that would be my key strategy to open Marks Jewelers and bring them on board as a fully active account. I went to my vault and reached for my three carat plus diamond box. I took out the following: Round Brilliant Cut, 3.65 carat, F color, VS1 clarity, certified by GIA. The diamond was truly a masterpiece cut and polished by one of the finest cutters in the world. Now, for the women reading this, you know exactly what this is. However, for the men, suffice it to say that every woman wants one, so go buy it for her. The diamond was spectacular and made more than an impressive presentation with its trade price tag of $55,000.00 . The plan was simple: Place the diamond in a special black velvet presentation box, take the stone up to Marks Jewelers, say absolutely nothing and place this stone in front of the owner with a note, written on company stationery, which read, "This inventory, and more like it, is a phone call and 45 miles away!"

Much like the magnificent diamond (well, almost), I thought the plan was flawless. It was a lateral, out of the box marketing scenario that I was convinced would cleverly communicate my intended message for me. I had no illusions at all that Marks Jewelers would actually buy the stone for inventory. I was not looking for a sale; I was looking for a memorable client contact that would concretize our business relationship and friendship. My "positive predatory" move was intended purely as a business development initiative designed to expand future transaction with this client. In general, there are literally a handful of retail jewelers who are either able or interested in buying a loose diamond of this caliber for inventory. My entire intention was to use it as a show-and-tell, exhibiting the level of loose diamond inventory that we at Kivi International, LLC were capable of supplying. I secured the diamond in my carry belt, grabbed a firearm (which many jewelers and diamond dealers have, and which I was fully licensed to own and carry) and jumped into my 1987 Mazda 626.

After picking up a warm drink for the ride, I settled into the car, placing a Zig Ziglar tape into the tape deck to continue listening to a series I was working through. It was another short road trip and a chance to study my "hunting territory" (and to see the USA), although it was tough to see anything, because everything was covered in mounds of this stuff the Americans call snow. But, I was in a good place and on the "hunt." I had everything I needed; oxygen in my lungs and my health, a $250.00 car that was still pushing strong at 150,000 miles on the clock, a family that loved me, a potential client ahead of me and one outrageous diamond with which to wow this client. I was still 10,000 miles away from home, but, in that moment, life was good, and I was so appreciative of the opportunity to "hunt." About ten miles out of Zelienople, I switched off the tape to gather my thoughts and prepare for my client approach. I was also particularly security conscious that day and wanted some quiet to fully engage all my senses. As I was coming into town, I began to do what all good "leopard" do -- role play the likely scenario, anticipating any twists and turns that might occur. I really thought this was going to be a no brainer – Mark would see this diamond and the note, look it over and respond with something like, "Mmm...very nice!... You have regular access to this kind of merchandise?... and, you are based in Pittsburgh?" I would very calmly and collectedly, in a matter of fact tone, answer, "Yeah, sure." -- incidentally messaging that the stone was actually not that impressive and was just a random sampling of our inventory holding in our Pittsburgh office. I would give off this, "Of course, we are a serious and significant loose diamond house" look, and Mark would give off this, "Well, I didn't know, but, now that I do, I will be calling you" look. And, the rest would be history! Mission accomplished, right? Wrong!

Study your "prey"; it will define your client approach and opportunity. Leopard do this, and, subsequent to the rest of the story below, this concept became incorporated into Leopardology™. Here is why!

Zelienople was a quaint town that apparently had an important regional history, reminders of which could be seen not only from the historical markers, but also from the abundance and complexity of railway tracks that greeted you coming into town. It was a less congested and suburban version of the many hamlets that surround Pittsburgh -- and just as old. Somehow, it was still the middle of winter and the gray weather and cold were just as awful as they were an hour and a half ago. I was "dialed in", to use a military term, and I was fully present and engaged in what I was doing and where I was. I was now downtown, which I could reach across, having located my client's store. Ever security conscious and aware, I did not slow down, but drove past it and round the block to make sure that I was not being followed. The store was indeed very impressive, beginning with the outside storefront and detail. It immediately communicated fine jewelry, generational trust and integrity and financial stability. It said all the right things to my brain, and, once I stepped inside, it only continued to reinforce my strategy. Now, I was really keen to further my relationship with this account and pull off my surefire client approach plan. Mark, the owner, was with a customer, but he had noticed me while I introduced myself to a store associate. We had met in Pittsburgh, previously, and I could tell that he recognized me. Beyond the fact that the last time there was an Orthodox Jew wearing a "yarmulke" (traditional head covering) in Zelienople, Pennsylvania, it was most likely Moses himself, Mark had heard my "vocal calling card," my South African accent. He briefly looked up and gave me a two finger wave, which I very warmly accepted from across his store. While waiting for my opportunity to see my client, I perused his beautifully appointed retail store. This was a modern, contemporary build out, well lighted and skillfully finished. The voice in my head told me that this was going to play out as the perfect "hunt." I could already hear my office phone ringing and Mark asking me for a particular significant loose diamond; I could already see Mark standing in the cutting factory in South Africa, on the trip I was going to take him on. This, I thought, was the "perfect" environment, the "perfect" scenario and the "perfect" client profile for my market offering.

Mark, the owner and principle jeweler, concluded his dealings with his customer and came over to me, extending his hand and greeting. He received me warmly and joked about my coming to the "hicks," conveying in an obvious tone that, surely, I was not there to sell diamonds! I was slightly thrown by that, but, as per my plan, I did not say a word. I was, however, thinking, "No, I just prefer to have my shirts dry cleaned in Zelienople." I was so married to my un-researched and preconceived notion of Marks Jewelers that I did not register this first hint of how mistaken I was. I shook Mark's hand warmly and smiled. I complimented him on his wonderful store, and merely said to him that I had something for him to see that would do all my "talking" for me. I executed the mission I had rehearsed in my head. I put my hand into my carry belt wallet, took out this gem quality 3.65 carat diamond in its unique presentation box and placed it on the counter in front of him. Before he could handle it, I reached into my prepared coat pocket, which housed my note and a diamond magnification loupe, both of which I placed immediately next to the stone. I said nothing. Mark first picked up the note and then glanced at the stone. He did not even pick up the diamond or the loupe but looked up at me and said, "Fifty to sixty thousand?" I shook my head in the affirmative giving him the "Uh-huh." I thought, "For sure, this is our tipping point; I am in and have made a strong client."

As he grabbed a pen and paper from the sales counter, Mark began to walk around the counter and towards a large window, indicating for me to follow him. I did, and we stood together looking out of his store onto and across the main street. He gestured to me to look out for a moment, and then asked me what I saw. Not sure at all where Mark was going with this, I repeated and affirmed his question, "What do I see?" Not wanting to share with him our family "funeral home décor" joke, I hesitantly said, "A small, West Pennsylvania town that would be attractive to people retiring and looking to get out of the rat race." Mark semi-smiled and said, "No, I mean…over on that side," pointing to a limited and distant, but visible, view of several industrial entities and activities. "It looks like a huge 84 Lumber operation and some kind of steel rolling and production mill," I said, as if back in 4th grade, hoping to give the teacher the correct answer. Mark shook his head in the affirmative and gave me an "Uh-huh," as he moved to a flat surface and wrote me the following note:

Nice stone. But, why would any of my clients want to give me almost two years' worth of their earnings to buy a diamond? I am not sure about South Africa, but here, the average salary in a steel mill or lumber yard is $30,000.00. Nice stone. Wrong client.

Mark smiled as he placed the note in my hand, as did I upon reading it. Aside from helping write this chapter of my book, Mark, the jeweler, had given me an invaluable and, quite frankly, irreplaceable lesson in the value of client study. While indeed there were a few wealthy retirees that occupied the town and its surrounding area, they were a very small percentage of his regular diamond buying clientele. They, their children and grandchildren, when visiting for holidays, were active browsers and buyers of finished jewelry and watches, but the largest percentage of his client customer base came from the workforce of the town itself. And this, I had missed entirely! They were engagement and bridal shoppers looking for a three to five thousand dollar price point, not a single round brilliant diamond that would retail somewhere in the region of $70,000.00. Yes, the store needed to facilitate the expectation and consumer wants of this niche population of wealthy retirees in the vicinity, but could certainly not depend on their occasional and seasonal business.

I stayed a short while, chatted with my "client," and learned more about his business and community. He was most kind in preventing me from feeling too embarrassed about my misreading of his business and true client base. Ultimately, he extended me the opportunity to communicate where we might be able to do some business, and what I could offer him in the way of inventory that he does sell. However, most powerfully, and with a touch of panache, he had graduated me from the "school of shmendrik" (beautiful Yiddish expression that, loosely explained, is the kindest way possible to use the word "fool")!

And, what a "shmendrik" I had been, having taken unnecessary risk and exposure in carrying such a valuable stone about hundred miles there and back, and having offered a prospective client a magnificent and impressive inventory holding of exactly the type of inventory he does NOT need! Beyond that, having purveyed to my client what was only, oh…ten times higher than the top end of his average store sale, I had shown him something extremely difficult to ever recover from -- ignorance. And, I had done it in the worst possible way, revealing a clear and unmistakable lack of understanding of his client base, customer pool and business model, an understanding, which I had taken great effort and preparation to exhibit in his very store. "Shmendrik".

Here's the thing friends: This entire episode could well have been avoided, and a much more successful and precise client approach could have been executed, had I just taken out ten minutes to study my client; to ask him about his business and customers; to research the area, the surrounding industry, the market place and the population; but, most importantly, to research my client; to get inside his store merely on a fact-finding mission; to speak to industry members who might know him and his business; to look at his advertising material and publicity; and, to study his buying habits, business and social behavior. Quickly, I would have been messaged about what Marks Jewelers actually does, and not what I wanted them to do. I would have designed my approach around **their** need and not **mine**. Study your client; it will accurately define your client approach opportunity.

Client Profits Start With Client Profiles...Ever Watch CSI?

In today's world, client research has never been easier and more accessible. While the internet, and the plethora of social network media, "supposedly" give us client networking efficiency, they also give us another invaluable commodity -- client study opportunity. Anywhere in the world and at any time, driven entirely by one's need, one can access a client's website, Plaxo or LinkedIn profile to gain abundant client information and intelligence. It is in front of us 24/7, and all we need to do is tap into it with "Forensic Sales Science" eyes!

The world of forensic science maintains that everything you need to know in order to solve a crime is left behind at the scene of the crime for trained eyes to gather. I have precisely the same theory with regards what I call "forensic sales science." I absolutely believe that everything one needs to prospect and close a client or leadership initiative is present at the "scene." It is with the client prospect, board, corporation or entity you are attempting to close and simply needs a pair of trained eyes to gather. Training one's eyes to perceive nuances and details of client entry intelligence is the key; one has to become a specialist **CSI** (**C**lient **S**cene **I**nvestigation) detective, to understand that, just as it is with you, a client's office, store, home or car, etc. is where he does his living. Here is the theory: If objects and surroundings can speak for the "dead" at a crime scene, then they can certainly do the same for the "living" at a client scene. Everything about us is a clue as to what goes on between our ears and in our hearts. It may not always be precise, because things out of context can be deceiving. But, if we learn to connect the dots and thread things together over a timeline, we can very clearly gain a sense and profile of our sales or leadership prospect. This will allow us to create an accurate client profile and design a strategic client approach that is unique.

That tiny Rotary Club lapel pin on his suit jacket, or that small pink breast cancer ribbon on her blouse, or that Private Pilot Association sticker on his car, or that Husky Owners Club of America key chain are all shouting out directions for a perfect "client" approach. But, your eyes have to be seeing, your ears listening and your brain connecting. For, if they are not, what good is it that your father-in law is the district governor of the Rotary Club, or that your mother is the chief government liaison for the Cancer Research Institute, or that you, yourself, are an avid amateur pilot, or that your company owner has a brother-in-law in Alaska who breeds award winning Husky dogs? You see my point? The bits and pieces of information you gather will come together to create a client profile that, itself, is full of tell-tale signs of what makes that client tick. Quite simply, the degree to which you can align your market offering with your prospect's profile is the degree to which you will close.

That "IKI" (I Knew It) Feeling We Get.

Leopard do this with such ease and without any apology. Unlike us, they have no qualm at all in choosing **not** to engage a particular client, or, alternatively, to specifically engage a particular client in a particular way. They unabashedly lead off on all "sales" and "leadership" initiatives based on what the "client" profile has told them. As we mentioned earlier, clients are not a one-size-fits all, and leopard intrinsically know this. A "client" either is an option for them, or it is not; it all depends on its profile. Now, here is something big! Once they have determined a "client" to be an option for them, they instinctively trust that the "client" itself holds the key to a successful "client" closure. Let's unpack that for a moment. If, based on our client study and client profile, a prospect falls within our gamut as a viable, feasible and acceptable risk-to-reward, then a further commitment to fully studying that client is what will get it closed. All one would need to know with regards the who, what, when and where of this prospect can be found by further study of this client; his exact need, his positioning in the market, his efficacy and history in the market, his proficiencies and deficiencies, his likes and dislikes, his philanthropy or lack thereof, his preferences and ambivalences, and his willingness or reluctance to do business with you. All of this information, in its verbal and nonverbal form, will come to answer that all important and singular question one will have: How do we make money with this client? The answer is nowhere else but with the very thing you already have – your client.

Of course, we all understand, but seldom practice, the discipline that it takes to refrain from dealing with certain clients. I am not suggesting that it is possible to have the same conviction and instinctive sense that leopard have in this regard; but, I am proposing that we learn to merely say "No" and believe in ourselves. "No" is "No" and does not always need finessed rhyme and reason or the logical deduction of intellectual fluency to be upheld. How many times in your own life can you recall an instant when your gut told you to say "no" but, regrettably, your "human power" of logical deduction could not find a reason for it, and you, therefore, said "yes" when you shouldn't have? How often do you hear, "I should have just said 'no'"? Well, why the heck didn't you? Here is why: You did not commit to the client profile that you had formulated; you did not have the discipline to respect the intelligence and information your client studying receptors had collated, which, as you may now recall, were messaging you – "No!" In fact, it is quite possible that they were "screaming" "No!" But, in your desire to gain client entry, you ignored it. It happens to all of us on various levels and is part of the human condition. Our need to be accepted and to get "in" and to "win" can often quiet even obvious indicators and client study information that so clearly articulate, "Do Not Touch!" In the analysis, it is not that we were not aware; it is more that we were aware and did it anyway. We convince ourselves otherwise with narratives like this: "If only I had known!" or "I didn't know!" or "How was I to know?" etc. Friends, we **do** know. And, we all **know** that we **do** know. We knew it at the time, because it was communicated to us by the client profile that our natural-profiling instinct had provided us. But, we chose to ignore it.

Acknowledging the power of our natural ability to formulate profiles, and then having the gumption to act on them, is an attribute and characteristic of result-centric and regular closers. Across the board, whether medical diagnosticians, truck drivers, senatorial legislators, captains of industry, corporate CEO's, homicide detectives, airline pilots or business entrepreneurs, following a hunch, or gut feeling, is, more often than not, responsible for their vocational success. It begins with an unequivocal awareness of, and adherence to, a prospect profile that their brain formulated, and that they then allowed to inform their decision making process. I know that you are entirely familiar with this, because you have experienced it. The opportunity before us is to convert the subliminal, subconscious messaging into regular and initiated behavior -- to use it as an asset, and to call it into active service on our "hunt" for success. Every client option has a profile: His world, his behavior and your interactions with him, offer you all that you need in order to formulate this profile. By becoming conscious to the process, instead of an unwitting participant, you substantially increase your close rate and dramatically lower your potential risk. Client profiling is a true gift and G-d's way of affording us a natural hedge against bad business and bad clients. Actively use it, and put it to work for you. Become an expert dot connector and increase your situational awareness of both the significant and the insignificant. Learn to observe the details, and value any opportunity to study your client and to get face time.

Subsequently, and this is where the wheels often fall off, you have to trust it. If your gut is telling you "yes," then it is a "yes," and you need to close it with everything you have; you must close with the equivalent of a complete "throat clutch close" that leopard so effectively use. However, if it is "no," then it needs to be "no" -- not a "no, but"; rather, a "no, period." Entrepreneurs, particularly, are always concerned that, if they do not reel in the fish they currently have hooked, they may not get another bite. There are two things they must know: Firstly, in time, they will get another bite; secondly, if their equipment is wrong for this current fish, they may destroy their ability to fish in the future. Are you with me here? There is a huge temptation to "do the business." However, when one ignores a client profile, one does so at one's peril. It can potentially be the deal that takes you down, that destroys your reputation, or that prevents the growth of your business. Client profits really do begin with client profiles -- so do client losses!

Tell Me Again...What Do We Do?

For all the times that I have been blessed and privileged to see lion, cheetah and leopard in the African bush, I have never seen any of them hunting with a manila "client" file under their arm. I am yet to see a leopard on the hunt for an impala with a printout of a Microsoft Notepad and/or jpeg photo of the impala. Why? So, I know you are thinking, "Come on, Kivi, don't be ridiculous; where are they supposed to put the file when they are running?" But, that is not the real reason they don't do this (especially considering that Office Depot has recently come out with the "attack pack," a feline predator version of the sleek, executive "sling pack" by Swiss Army). So, they clearly have options for carrying a "client" file, photos and all sorts of notes and client details, yet they choose not to. Why not? Well, what if I suggested to you that it might just jeopardize their effectiveness on the hunt and result in an incomplete "client" capture! Huh!? Ok, stay with me here for a moment.

Leopard are entirely "client" focused and imbued with an undisturbed ability to remain totally focused and attached to the hunt. When leopard hunt, there is no question as to why they are hunting and what it is they are hunting. There is truly little, if anything, that can derail them from the "result" they are looking to achieve, because they are result-centric and not process-centric. Also, they don't watch the morning business news.

On occasion, it is the courage to just stay in the "hunt," which has scored us our big clients: More often, however, it is a resolute clarity of the mission objective that has done it. Think about it; there is a difference between them. The latter is an unwavering and unapologetic relationship we have with the result of what we are doing, not with how we are doing it. I am referring to something that transcends the self-esteem required to believe in oneself and one's ability to "do it." I am referring more specifically to that mental resilience that gives us the intellectual "permission" and eligibility to go out there and successfully make a loyal and profitable client, in spite of outside opposition. To do this, one has to be "hunting" clients, not customers. This means closing a client prospect in a process that moves beyond client details and information in a manila file. (That's for making a customer.) You gather information and clearly identify a need, which you meticulously write down and analyze; you then simply respond to it by providing your service and discharging your contractual obligation to customer satisfaction. Customers are plentiful and do not require much skill or professionalism to get. (Think I'm kidding; think about some business people you know with personalities that shouldn't allow them to have oxygen in their lungs, let alone customers.) No, I am talking about clients -- willing and able parties, looking to transact with you and engage you in a friendship and business relationship that will result in mutual benefit and profit! That's a client -- an entirely different "animal," (Forgive me, I couldn't resist.), an entirely different level of transaction from that with a customer. Oh, make no mistake; the customer is an invaluable and indispensable component of the business process. However, please understand that customers will pay your bills, but clients will pay your profits!

In a client transaction, there is a true transfer of the essence of who you are as a human being, and the point of that transfer and its reception is what we loosely call a "close." The signature, paperwork and particulars that finalize the details are really just recording mechanisms that document that this transfer has taken place. But, the truly successful making and closing of a client onto one's books is a real science and can only happen if the parties are present in their entirety, well beyond the paperwork and details. There is no one, two or ten specific things that have to be "done" in order to please this client; one cannot refer to notes and paperwork, looking for what needs to be "done" next in order to discharge an obligation. A client relationship, much like any real relationship, is beyond that, and is not subject to the fulfillment of one or several things that must be "done." Rather, it is the very contact and connection itself; the very relationship in its entirety; the whole, big, macro picture. It is the delivery of everything you are and have to offer, not a compartmentalized excerpt of yourself that you have made notes of in a file.

And so, while on the "hunt" for a client, having anything separate one from the clarity of the mission objective can result in an incomplete capture. One may land up with a customer and not a client. Now, worse things have happened, but here is my point: In a consolidated, competitive global economy like ours, return-on-investment and the efficiency of the "hunt" is everything. The feasibility and viability of everything, including the time we spend out of the office and in front of prospects, is under scrutiny. The fact of the matter is that the return-on-investment from a customer cannot compare to that of a client. Leopard evidently understand this intrinsically, as they seldom make "customers" but seem to regularly make "clients." Welcome to "Nature-Nomics 101."

Study your client: Formulate a precise client approach, and do a lot more than pay your bills -- Make a client!

Chapter 10

You Have To "Leopard Crawl" Before You Can Walk!

Positive Predatory Pillar ™ No. 5

In the bush:

Hunt your hunt: If all the exact criteria necessary for a successful hunt are not in place, leopard will abandon the hunt and live to hunt another day.

Sell *you*, not what you think *you* should be.

My youngest, and like her sisters, beautiful and precious daughter was to be born in two weeks from the day, and so she was. It was November and summer in South Africa. My wife was, of course, at home in Johannesburg, organizing the house and preparing to give birth. Her husband, who shall remain nameless, was deep in the renowned and treacherous, raw but beautiful and extremely remote, Mohalenyane Plateau in the mountain kingdom of Lesotho, Africa. Now, why he was there, two weeks before his wife was to give birth, is truly the subject of another book, or two. However, the fact is that I and four friends spent three days, lost, deep in one of sub-Saharan Africa's most remote, dangerous and harsh regions. This included a Saturday, which, for an Orthodox Jew and Sabbath observer, became most interesting. But, given the potentially life threatening scenario that the five of us found ourselves in, we kept on moving. It would turn out that we were 100 kilometers from any form of western civilization, and in some trouble, if mild dehydration, three broken ribs, two broken fingers and a major infection setting in on two toes, whose nails had been torn off, qualify. (And that was just me.) No water, no food, no medical supplies and no way to call for help were minor issues, which only complicated matters further. It will not do it justice to explain to you, in brief, how I and my traveling companions landed up in this position, but we very much did. What I can share with you is that, unbeknownst to us at the time, we were about to experience an episode in our lives that would make "Survivorman" or "Man vs. Wild" on the Discovery Channel look like a 4ᵗʰ of July picnic.

We had been away from our base since 5:00 am, and it was about 10:00 am when our ordeal began to unfold. By midday, the temperature was somewhere around 38 degrees Celsius, (100 degrees Fahrenheit), and the mountain walls and rock terrain of the Mokhokhong Valley offered little shade. The sweltering African sun was draining precious water out of us and asking our muscles to think about shutting down. We were now on foot and totally lost to the world. While our family members knew that we were in the general region, it would have taken a search party weeks, if ever, to find what would have been five needles in a haystack. Our research had told us that there were some villages of the Nkoeng People that lightly inhabited this region, but we had no idea where. (Incidentally, Nkoeng means "place of large leopards"!) The only way out would be to mentally and physically engage the100 kilometer trek ahead; we would have to make our way through the perilous, and seemingly endless, miles of 10 inch foot paths that were supported by sheer cliff walls and that, at some points, dropped off to 1,000 feet below. We had a topography map, which told us that the river gorge was basically our guide and our only hope of surviving out there – period. But, while its waters were cool, they also had bilharzias (disease causing parasites) and were not safe for drinking. It was a mental game and an emotional roller coaster of literally climbing one mountain only to descend down it and into the river gorge. We would then cross the river, which at some points was riddled with hydraulics and under cuts, and ascend the next monster mountain right in front of us. We would use the river to rest and to provide the occasional quick protein fix of whatever was possible. (And no, bugs and insects are not kosher, but are permissible if one's life depends on it). Although surrounded by red rock and cliffs on either side, there was always the possibility that the river was home to crocs, and, most unlikely, but, perhaps, even hippos. There is an old African expression that the colorful Ndebele People of the southeast region of South Africa use: "Never trust a river in Africa." By midnight, the temperature would approach 5 degrees Celsius (41 degrees Fahrenheit), and, while we had to prepare for this, it was the least of our problems. We could make shelters and find cover. We also had two boxes of matches between us, and there was plenty of fire making material and suitable brush that would quickly light. As the sun set, we managed the sudden onset of the mountain wind, which became more and more biting, by using the rock crevasses, outcrops and overhangs for shelter. It was great natural protection against the elements and might even have gotten us through the night. One problem! There is a venomous snake that is spread throughout Southern Africa, but which is particularly abundant in the rock ledges and crevasses of, (you guessed it), Lesotho. Known as the puff adder, this short and puffy, but highly dangerous, snake is simply referred to by the locals as "noga," which just means "snake." This is a very large fanged, highly powerful, cytotoxic venomous snake, whose bite can be fatal unless treated within one to two hours. I was aware of this and particularly concerned about it, because we had no anti-venom with us or any means of communication. Puff adders are diurnal hunters in the mountain kingdom of Lesotho and tend to live in precisely the exact environment we were in -- rock formations, ledges and sandy foot paths that offer shelter and cover. Oh, by the way, so do several other species of venomous snakes, scorpions, baboons, hyena and, yes, leopard. Legend has it that, at one time, there were large lion prides in these parts, however, while there have been lion sightings in these mountains and valley crescents, lion would not have been our concern: Leopard and snake, and in that order, certainly were. Voted the wildlife expert by the group, it became my job to manage our safety from that perspective. It was about fire, noise, staying together and...prayer.

The night brought on a darkness that was almost palpable. There was no moon, and the explosion of the clear, starlit sky was our only light beyond the bundle torches and fire we had made. The terrain was so mountainous that everything offered prime cover and hiding for all sorts of things that could, quite simply, kill you. Those "things" also had the upper hand, because we humans had a five to ten foot visibility -- and were very cold. The situation was not great, to say the least, and we were edgy and exposed. We sat for a while on the top of a valley peak to get some perspective and think tank the plan. We decided that, notwithstanding the night cover and its inherent dangers, we needed to move off the mountain walls and down into the valley grass land; there, at least, we could only be killed by the famed Cape cobra. The thinking was that we would have more environment control and less exposure in what we knew was the exact, known, local territory of the feared puff adder snake; we would also be in a better position to see approaching leopard and hyena. Descending these rock cliff mountains during the day was dangerous; at night it was "bloody stupid," as we like to say in South Africa. We were faced with sharp, angular rock paths giving us a footing of loose, red rock gravel and sandstone with sudden drops of 5, 10 and 15 feet. You may as well just break your ankle before you start, but, it was the decision we took for our safety, and off we went. It took us some three hours to come into the valley, but not before one of my friends had dislocated his shoulder falling onto a termite mound. It was now after midnight. We came together in a thick grass patch where we regrouped for a "bos-beraad" (Afrikaans for bush meeting). We somewhat got our bearings and rested. It was extremely cold, and, in the dark, it was almost impossible to establish our position relative to the river line. We had a little fire going, which provided some light in our immediate vicinity. As best we could tell, we were not far off from the Mkhomazana River, although, because of the high winds, we could not hear it. We sat a while and then discussed options. We made the decision to stay put for the night, using tree branches and brush to make shelter and some cover against the wind. While I was scouting our exact position for risk exposure to leopard and hyena, two of the others went to get fire wood.

I felt we were best off staying in the center of the valley. There were pros and cons. The center of the valley was ripe with tall, long, lush grass and was most exposed to the wind; however, it offered the most visibility. Trees were not a possibility for cover, as they were too small and scattered apart. The periphery of the valley offered lots of rock outcrops and natural cover, but no visibility of what, when or from where something might be coming at you. As well, there were significant drop offs that made ideal ambush sites for leopard. It was going to be the center of the valley. We would create a circular area, flatten the grass land and build shelter and fire, staying in close proximity to each other. Using boot laces, I tied two empty Coke cans we had to the end of a stick, making a noise generator which would scare oncoming predators…we hoped.

As I, and one of my friends, began preparing our camp site, we heard our two friends who were collecting fire wood calling out. They were not even visible to us and were far over on the edge of the valley perimeter, but we could hear them shouting "…fire!…fire!…" We made our way over to them following their lit torches; never before was the word "fire" so sweet to hear. Down the valley, way off, barely visible, but visible nonetheless, at a distance of three or four kilometers, we could see what looked like flickering of fire. People! A village! Civilization! We would survive and see our families again! We just had to get to this village. We were elated and reenergized. Immediately, we abandoned all other plans, as we prepared to follow the "light."

As we were ready to pull out, it was I who stopped the group for a moment and reminded them that "civilization" means different things to different people, and that we were in Basohtoland, place of the last known African cannibal tribe of Raboshabane. (Chief Raboshabane and his followers had turned to eating human flesh after the severe drought and famine of the early 1800's.) If that is a Basohto village, and we do make it there alive, who is to say they will be happy to receive us and keep it that way? There was a brief pause, while we all thought for a moment, after which I posed the option of taking our chances and staying put. I was outvoted, and we began our treacherous trek towards what, we hoped, was not a last remaining Raboshabane tribal village, where we might be greeted by a witch doctor and huge cauldron of boiling water.

Three hours later at approximately 3 o'clock in the morning, we arrived at the gates of the village, which had two burning lanterns on either side of the entrance. Yes, it was like taking a scene out of the original Indiana Jones movie! Now folks, there is good and bad news.

The good news is that the huge boiling cauldron that the witch doctor made us sit around for twenty minutes, while she removed all our evil spirits, was not for us. The bad news was that these very hospitable and welcoming people, with whom we could not communicate at all, were, in fact, descendants of the Raboshabne people that had adopted some Roman Catholic traditions from the early missionaries. You never thought you would hear an Orthodox Jew thank G-d for Roman Catholics, but I did. After an hour, or so, of being stared down by the entire village of some 150 members, we bartered our blood soaked and filthy under shirts and socks for a night's shelter, which they graciously extended us in their village shrine. They offered to slaughter a goat in our honor, but we declined the gift in exchange for any form of drinking fluids and medical attention. Liquid substance, (which contained some water and who knows what else), in dry hollowed out butternut squash gourds, hydrated us, and we slept in the shrine for the next three or so hours. Each one of us were given two "spiritual warriors" that slept near us, while the witch doctor, who was a female, sprayed water on us and recited prayers for our well being. We all "slept" with one eye open! (Look out for the book, or catch up with me at a corporate or public speaking engagement to find out how and when we got home alive!)

But, for now, let me share the following fascinating component of Leopardology™ that was born out of this experience. I was the first one up - not that I really slept a wink, awakened by, you got it, a rooster. I was suffocating from the lack of fresh air and smoke that filled the entire village. As I scrambled up, my body reminding me of my injuries, I noticed our "spiritual warriors" were gone. I was wrong, they had just relocated outside the hut/shrine, standing guard and awaiting our emergence. I came outside, and, even with my broken ribs, toes and finger, I could not help but marvel at the view that greeted me. It was simply stunning. The village was perched on a peak, surrounded by lush green fields that were worked for agriculture. The view was panoramic and breathtaking. (Incidentally when you have three broken ribs, everything is literally "breathtaking.") But, this truly was magnificent. The young warriors quickly pointed me towards an elder gentleman dressed in traditional garb, sitting on a ledge that overlooked this incredible scenery. He was a village elder, and he actually spoke Afrikaans, which allowed me to communicate with him. I paid my respects to him and immediately went to get the others. This was more than good! We now had a senior village member who knew this region like the back of his hand and a common language in which to communicate. I returned to him, while the others were getting themselves together, and had a few minutes of conversation alone with him. The very first thing he said to me was in the form of a statement and question as follows:

The leopard here in Mokhokhong valley are large and strong. They have killed our goats and even our people. At night, did you stay out of the valley grass and keep on the sandstone paths and rock ledges of the mountain?....

I shook my head in the negative and said to him that, before we found his village, which kindly took us in, we had descended the mountain ridges and were going to spend the night on a valley grass clearing we had made. I explained to him our brilliant logic regarding the puff adder snake and regarding visibility of the leopard. The wise and time tested old man, whose name was Tlabakela, chuckled and said the following to me:

My friend, people will tell you that the puff adder is lazy and shy, and that the leopard in these parts stays mostly on the rock ledges and outcrops... My friend, it is better to believe that the adder is lazy and shy in the mountains than to believe that a leopard will not be hunting, crawling on his belly in the grass lands of the valley...

There is not a special operations unit in the world that has not trained its members in it, and it is even called by its generic name – the leopard crawl. It is an amazing phenomenon and behavior of all felines, but, without question, the award goes to leopard for their proficiency and excellence in using the leopard crawl -- that extraordinary ability to crouch down, remaining unnoticed, and stalk their prey undetected. While other big cats, like lion for example, can also be seen "leopard crawling," they use it predominantly to set up and position the hunt prior to a full deployment of the hunting pride. It allows them to remain undetected by their prey, as well as by competitor predators, during this set-up phase. Leopard, however, use it much more specifically as an integral part of their "closing" strategy; they use it to remain undetected by their "client" prospect, enabling them to get within five to eight feet of that prospect entirely unnoticed. This dramatically influences their "close rate." Unless the hunt resulted from an unexpected and sudden opportunity, or from a tree ambush (by which leopard strike their prey from the limb of a tree), there is not a leopard hunt that has, or will, go down without the use of the "leopard crawl." It is an extraordinary asset and resource within their "organization"; why would they ever hunt without deploying it?

Very often, and without remorse, leopard will actually abandon the hunt, unless all the exact criteria for a successful hunt are in place. There is an instinctive "no go" barometer that leopard have, which allows them to disengage a hunt that they feel is either unsafe or unlikely to be successful. Boy! Don't we all wish we had one of those, telling us what we should or should not pursue? This is a fundamental aspect of hunt efficiency and return-on-investment that leopard display. The famous "leopard crawl," for example, is a hugely successful and critical component of the leopard hunt. If there are conditions that do not allow for its deployment, leopard are likely to abandon the hunt. Conversely, if conditions do allow for its deployment, there is an instinctive and intrinsic commitment to its full and complete use. Leopard have an acute, instinctive understanding that "Hunting **Your** Hunt" is not just a good idea, but rather, the key to an exceptionally high close rate and success as a species.

Tlabakela, the tribe elder, was not the only one to have said it to me that day. There was no doubt at all that the collective village wisdom was this: Leopard will always "**hunt their hunt**" and do what leopard do best. Here is what they were communicating: The incredible "leopard crawl" is one of those things leopard do best. They were telling us to stay out of the valley grass and keep up on the rock ridges, not because we wouldn't encounter leopard on the rock ridges -- we might! However, if leopard have an option between limited "leopard crawl" on the mountain ridges and boundless "leopard crawl" through the grassland of the valley -- well, they will opt to "hunt their hunt" in the grasslands, where their unique "leopard crawl" can be used to its maximum, greatly increasing their chance for success. Leopard always "hunt **their** hunt" using the specific tools they have been given to do so. In the jungles of commerce, as we "hunt" for success, we should do the same, each of us using **our** unique, specific tooling and personalities to close and secure clients.

Put Your Elbows On The Table And Eat With Your Paws!

Watching leopard eat is not for the faint hearted. This is so of most carnivores, but is especially so of leopard, and for good reason. The first time I was privileged to see this in the wild, I was ten years old, in the bush with my family on our annual safari vacation that was part of our education. My father had spotted a leopard up in a tree with an impala kill. It was a fairly unobstructed sighting, and, with the use of binoculars, one could clearly see this huge leopard tearing away at its meal. Having four older sisters and one younger put me way down in the pecking order for use of one of the two pairs of very expensive binoculars. As the "bino's" made their way past my two elder sisters, all I could hear were these animated cries of: "Ooooh...sick!!...disgusting...ooooh... sick!!..." Once I heard that, I immediately had to see this and simply could not wait my turn. I just thought "Girls"..., which, growing up with five sisters, is something I often thought. Immediately, I jumped into the front of the family van next to my father, who got permanent "dad rights" on the other pair of binoculars, and did the father-and-son thing. In seconds, I was fixed up with a pair of powerful game viewing binoculars. I locked in and focused on this incredible sight. I cried out, "Ooooh...sick!!"

It looked like the deleted autopsy scenes they don't show you from the television show, "Dr. G, Medical Examiner." Here is why! Leopard have extraordinarily powerful jaws, teeth, facial and neck musculature. Their tongues have tiny, razor-blade sharp, barb-like nodules on them that are supported by extremely strong tongue muscles. And, their paws and claws need no introduction. As you know by now, leopard are solo, solitary hunters, and, beyond having to "close clients" alone, they have to "retain them for profit" alone. They do not have the conglomerate resources of many heads -- in this case, many heads with teeth in them.

When a pride of lion, for example, "close" a large wildebeest or buffalo, the sheer number of teeth and claws that make contact with that "client" will soften it up and allow older and younger members "easy meat" access. The power of the pride, just in its numbers, will naturally make sure that the "client" is fully maximized, and that all legitimate profit is taken. Leopard, however, do not have this available to them; they have, therefore, been equipped with tooling and apparatus that compensates for their solitary nature. All this equipment, and more, comes together to produce one of the most efficient, effective and "Ooooh...sick!!" eating machines on earth. It is an unapologetic "get in there and rip that thing to shreds because I can" thing that is executed with strategic precision. As leopard handle their prey, they incidentally prepare it for eating, but it is their total and unabashed commitment to using the full strength and gamut of their feeding apparatus that allows them to "savor" the sweet taste of complete "client profit."

Young cubs and sub-adults are taught from an early age to continually groom, clean and sharpen this equipment. Not only does it teach them to keep it in good working order for maximum usage, but it also serves to message them as to the very existence of this equipment. As we have discussed previously, unlike us humans, leopard instinctively know that everything they need for success, they have. It's all with them and on them. At all times, they carry all the equipment and apparatus necessary for total success. Unlike us, leopard travel light with only their original "factory issue" equipment -- not because they do not know better, but, rather, because they do. Let me ask you this: Why don't leopard carry cell phones? I mean, in concept, this could dramatically **enhance** their hunt, their communication with their cubs and their territory management. Especially with Google Map, Weather Channel and calculator options, their prey location, terrain conditions and prey weight assessment would just be so much easier! (Don't forget the built-in camera and video for "Study Your Territory," "Know Your Prey," and "Study Your Competitor," the "Pillars of Positive Predatory Thinking" TM!) Still pictures and video would be invaluable in analyzing a "market." And hey, SMS and texting menus provide silent communiqué, perfectly in sync with leopard behavior. So, nu...what's the problem here? There is cellular reception all over the African bush, and, where there is not, there is satellite. Well, it's not what you think! The phone is not the problem for the leopard. No, it is the carry case and accessories that become complicated. It's all the "stuff" one has to have in order to support the "stuff" that supports the "stuff" that makes us much more **efficient** and **enhances** our "hunt" for success. It moves against leopard's instinctive common sense. In order for something to be an enhancer of their abilities, and not a detractor, it has to be low maintenance and allow them to "travel light." You see, here is the problem with leopard's using cell phones: Where would they charge it?

Well, electrical outlets are difficult to come by in the African bush, so the best option would be a special long-life battery with a car charger. In order to get a car registered, however, leopard would have to produce a current emission test clearance; in order to do that, they would have to obtain insurance on the car. But, as we all know, insurance is ridiculously expensive if you are under 25. However, if you maintain good grades at school, it is possible to get a discounted rate with companies like Geico Insurance. However, Geico needs verification from a school about your grades. Now, you have to walk about 1000 kilometers a day, back and forth, to a recognized school. Because of the extreme difficulty this poses, you decide to register for a charter cyber school and "home school," except that you need an electrical outlet to re-charge your laptop to get on line. You can, however, go to Radio Shack and buy a car charger converter, but that will not help you, because you can't get a car for the above stated reason. It is now clearly evident that, as a leopard in the African wild, you simply cannot survive without a car. Period! So you go with the **only** option you have; walk the 1,000 Kilometers to and from school every day, so that you can get verification of your good grades, so that you can get a discount from Geico Insurance, so that you can afford the car insurance, if you are under 25. The enormous inconvenience of all this "stuff" that needs to happen in order to have what is needed to charge the cellular phone is complicating the leopard's life and is consuming huge amounts of time, preventing him from hunting. So friends, you see, carrying a cell phone, the very thing I proposed to enhance their hunt will actually detract from it. This is why leopard do not carry cell phones!

There is, also, not a special operations unit in the world that has not been trained in "traveling light." But, as defined by the leopard, this does not mean throwing off unnecessary weight that will slow you down. Rather, developing a "travel light" mentality within the context of Leopardology™ is about a true understanding that less is more. You have it, and it is with you. It is visceral knowledge that nothing will enhance your performance more than the full and complete utilization of that which you already have. Why? The reason is that it has been custom built and designed with G-dly perfection that will work for your requirement like nothing else will. Identify the unique and exclusive elements of **your** "hunt," (your specific leadership, customer relationship, selling and closing features), and have them deploy and mobilize in every single "hunt" you attempt. Hunt **your** hunt; that is your market differentiator and the thing that your clients are buying. You will never see a leopard hunting like a crocodile from under the water! Hunt **your** hunt.

Hunting On Purpose!

To watch a leopard hunt unfold is to watch conviction, dedication and purpose in motion. In a world where ADD has become as common as ABC, the leopard's hunt is a bastion of unrelenting perseverance and commitment to a focused result. Everything about the hunt, and I mean every move and every thought, is precise and intended. Nothing is random and nothing is left to chance. Take a look at something. Leopard have four legs with four paws – right? Ok, so when they hunt, leopard will place their two back paws precisely in the paw prints that were created by their two front paws. Are you with me here? This is incredible to see. When you track leopard that are hunting, (a true death wish), you will, in fact, see only two paw prints, not because they have only two legs, but because the two back paws have been placed exactly in the prints of the front two. This is a genius ruse that leopard use to throw off other predators, like hyena and lion, that may be following the hunting leopard. Guess what? It really works! Total confusion reigns, and trailing predators often back off because of the complexities this trick creates.

While G-d's genius, as it manifests in nature, is His way of saying "Hi!...I am over here...," the point I wish to communicate is a different one. In our "hunt" for viable and profitable business, we so often develop a laissez-fare attitude towards our very ability to "hunt." I am not referring to burn-out or a lack of passion for the "hunt" or for what we are doing. Rather, I am getting at the idea that we forget that we even have the ability to "hunt" at all. Of course by "hunt," I am referring to the distinct human ability to intellectually conceive, originate and create an idea, concept or initiative and actually bring it to fruition. We are "hunters" of social, communal, political and business opportunities and prospects. The fact is that we human beings have been equipped and tooled with all sorts of intellectual and physical genius to do so. I am really saying this: Leopard instinctively know that they have been created to "hunt" and have no problem at all doing so with conviction -- and on purpose!

Here is my rhetorical question for all of us business entrepreneurs, managers and community leaders. Why do **we**?

Why Leopard Don't Kill Grown Elephant!

On the one hand, we tell our kids that **everything** is possible, if you want it badly enough. On the other hand, we teach our children not to place a square peg in a round hole. Well, Adults, which one is it? Is all possible without limitation, or are things specific and particular to design? Positive Predatory Pillar No. 4, "Hunt **Your** Hunt", is here to submit to you that everything is **not** possible. In my humble opinion, it is a fallacy and misrepresentation that society has promoted, specifically to its youth. This might well explain how we are now living through one of the most confused periods of human civilization -- certainly one of the unhappiest. Never before in human history have we had more "stuff," and yet, arguably, never before has society as a whole been more miserable and disagreeable with each other. This is not born from the commonly thought "stress" of modern day living: It is born from confusion, a confusion and misrepresentation of what truly is possible and what truly is not!; what is real and what is not!; what is within my grasp and what is not!

I am a patriotic, law abiding and peace loving citizen of the United States of America, who values, beyond most, the freedom and liberty that true democracy offers. I have now had the unique privilege in my life to have voted in the two historic elections of both Nelson Mandela and Barak Obama. I support our current president, Barak Obama, and pray for his personal and national success, so that we, the people, the nation and the world, may be successful. However, (and I pray to be entirely incorrect), the study of Leopardology™ informs me that his popularity and celebrity will be short-lived, and here is why. While campaigning, President Barak Obama very definitely communicated "Yes we can." However, the campaign did not complete the end of the sentence and left millions with the following question: "Yes we can... **do what?**" Leopardology™ submits that, when anything and everything is offered as a possibility, we are really being offered confusion and speculation. When we introduce definitive ideas and complete the sentence, "Yes we can **do 'so and so'**...," we are offered understanding and clarity. So often, when everything is a possibility, nothing is a possibility. Many times the lack of productivity or efficacy in the business world is due to a lack of clarity regarding what is genuinely achievable -- and what is not.

Please do not throw out the baby with the bath water here and read this as a political commentary. It is not, and it does not seek to make either a Republican or Democratic statement. I seek only to underscore and emphasize a critical understanding of what it means to truly "hunt your hunt." Leopard instinctively do this. They have an uncanny ability to know, well before the risk exposure to the hunt is assumed, exactly what "client" options are within their ability to "close and retain" -- and which are not. At all costs, unless they are defending their lives, leopard will not step outside of this place of clarity. They will refuse to engage the "confusion," even if sold to them with glitz and glamour, because it might just get them killed. I often hear people talking about society's biggest killer, cancer, as the "big C." But, I submit to you that the "big C" is Confusion and is a bigger killer of success than cancer will ever be. It is a "killer" of happiness, feasibility, reality, viability and the accurate understanding of what we, as humans, truly can or cannot achieve. Do not get me wrong: Dream big...No, dream huge! Forget the moon; reach beyond the stars, but keep your feet on the ground. Genuinely know what you, as a human being, can accomplish, and pursue it. Because, here is the thing: When you get to the moon that you have so passionately reached for, you will discover that you cannot naturally breathe.

In our social world and in our commercial world, we have ignored clarity at the price of confusion. We have accepted and tolerated financial, commercial and market confusion in the name of political and social correctness. The market correction and vitalization of our global economies will not come in the form of a stimulus package. It will come in the slow, but certain, unraveling of decades of exposure to the "big C" -- confusion that has ravaged our social insides and created huge tumors of "stuff" that we have consumed, believing it would enhance our "hunt" for success. We will gradually see a return of market fundamentals, not in the way economists use the term, but in the way leopard do. We will see a return to the "natural," fundamental principles that our grandparents and great grandparents intrinsically knew to be correct; clarity over confusion, reality over idealism, achievability over feel-good sentiment, and feasibility over public recognition. We will revert to a local and global economy in which corporations are not all things to all people, offering all possibilities. Businesses and their proprietors will complete the sentence "Yes we can…" with an articulation of exactly what it is they can do. **Clarity** will become a valued commodity, selling to clear minded consumers, who perceive its value and are willing to pay for it.

Hunt **Your** Hunt.

Chapter 11

The New Global Economy Will Be Old!

Positive Predatory Pillar ™ No. 5

In the boardroom:

Hunt your hunt: If all the exact criteria necessary for a successful hunt are not in place, leopard will abandon the hunt and live to hunt another day.

Sell *you,* not what you think *you* should be.

LONG BEFORE TECHNOLOGY and the web allowed one to portray oneself as something he or she was not, it has been a human tendency for people to sell themselves to their communities and clients as something other than who and what they really are. It is a deep-seated ailment of man that promotes the idea that anything is better than the original. I recently had the opportunity to speak for a global sales and leadership team from the Honda motorcycle corporation. In preparing for my keynote, my research on the company taught me many interesting and impressive facts. However, it was something I learned from interviewing one of their executives in their South American markets that fascinated me most. While Honda is one of the most trusted and reliable automotive brands in the world, almost 35% of their revenue in certain markets, and within certain categories, is generated from after-market and post-production products and services. In other words, almost one out of three people, who buy a Honda product in this category, will buy other "stuff" that is not part of the standard factory issue in order to "enhance" their experience. Let's be clear here: These are not just accessories such as apparel, seat covers and chain protectors that do not impact performance; these are things, gadgets and gizmos that, supposedly, directly interact with various aspects of performance, thereby "enhancing" it. Incidentally, I own a Honda off road motorcycle in its original factory form: It is as reliable and responsive as the day I bought it.

If one stops for a moment to digest this information, it is incredible to comprehend. It is mind-boggling to process that a secondary industry and market, which supports the human notion that good is not good enough, and which facilitates the enhancement of an already excellent product, is as profitable and almost the same size as the primary market itself. Wow! This could only work in the human world. Nature would never tolerate such a flagrant statement of rejection of the quality and efficacy of a well-designed, well-equipped and well-engineered product.

This is something that has crept into almost every industry, every aspect of business dialog and every global commercial conversation. The sheer speed of technology production has allowed for a certain "disposable" and "insufficient" attitude to develop. Products, services and people are expected to simply be deficient and incomplete on arrival. By the time a product gets to you, or is shipped to your office, a new version, model or bundle is already available and considered a "must have" for success. There is always something else, other than the thing you have in front of you right now, that will work just a little bit better. In our commercial psyche today, it is perfectly acceptable to say things like: "I just bought it, and it's already outdated…."; or, "I just got this, but I heard they are coming out with…."; or, "When I get the next one, I will be able to…." Excusing performance on technology, product or service has become quite the norm in all sectors of society. Moreover, the lack of human performance and aptitude has become entirely excusable based on insufficient "stuff." Hey, what happened to the childhood maxim we all grew up with: "Bad craftsman always blame their tools."? Today we live in a world where a terminated, disgruntled employee can fight a dismissal in court on the grounds that an employer failed to replace Windows XP with Vista on his office desktop. I am kidding, of course, but you get my point. We live in a world where "Tools Maketh the Man." Leopardology™ suggests that

160

"G-d Maketh the Man, Complete."; "Man, with G-d's Help, Maketh Tools to Help Man, Not Replace Man." This is fun and light, yet, herein lies the fundamental difference between one's believing that one **has** all one needs to be successful, or the alternative belief that one must **get** what one needs to be successful. Leopard instinctively live in a space that dictates that they **have** what they need to be successful.

Tools help, but never replace. So often, and with such frequency, entrepreneurs, managers, CEO's and leaders with great ideas, great initiatives and great client prospects that hold tremendous promise, "tool" themselves right out of business. Correct, they get so caught up in "getting" what they think they need to be successful, that they distance themselves from the core activity and focus of being successful. Hold on, before you use my book as fire paper, let's be clear here: I am not advocating we revert to "Archimedes Screw" and ignore all advances that have offered us human beings tools of efficiency and efficacy. Stay with me, please: I am advocating that we acknowledge them for exactly what they are -- tools -- just tools that have offered us better, quicker and more effective delivery of our **inherent proficiencies** -- not a replacement **for** them! This is the key component of Leopardology™ that is presented by "Hunt Your Hunt."

If we were to eavesdrop on what mom leopard says to her sub-adult youngster heading out on his or her first hunting expedition of a 125 pound impala in the African bush land, it would sound something like this:

"Honey, Dad and I are so proud of you, and we love you unconditionally. By all means, pay a visit to Dick's Sporting Goods and buy all the camouflage products you can find. Get online and visit HuntingKnives.com, and, please, order in the best Japanese, sharpened and hand crafted, surgical steel blade hunting knife money can buy. But, Honey, here is the message your father and I want you to always remember: Do not forget about what G-d gave you. Do not forget to get down in the grass and use your natural body camouflage to crawl undetected to within five feet of your "client." Then use your three inch canine teeth that bite through steel to "close, sign and seal" your "client" in total silence. And then, Sweetheart, use those razor sharp claws and massive paws you have to put all that tree climbing you

*have practiced to good use. With all that muscle you have in your shoulders, tree your "client" and "retain" it for "profit" in peace and quiet. Good luck, Honey -- we **know** you can do this -- you **have** what it takes. We love you, Honey."*

Forget about the school tuition and cost of travel and lodging. Take a look at what you or your parents spent on just the "stuff" that you or your kids needed to go to college.

I cannot tell you how many times I have gone into corporations, organizations and associations in a Leopardology™ consultancy capacity, only to find this exact issue at the core of what is creating lethargic and sluggish performance results. In a feeding frenzy, generated by the need to survive and uphold numbers in this global economic consolidation, business entities are scrambling to get what they are being told they **need** to compete in the "hunt." Time and time again, I see it across the board and around the world: Leadership and management urgently survey critical departments, such as HR, IT, accounting, and sales and marketing, desperately seeking to learn what they **need** to stay in the "hunt" and close deals. In turn, they scramble back to their "teams," who point out all the current **needs** that are preventing performance and who indicate where the cuts can take place in order to pay for the "**need fulfillment.**" Once the **need** is met and supplied, it is assumed that they will be back in the "hunt" in a meaningful and significant way. All too often, of course, they are not -- for obvious reason! They have distanced themselves from the core "hunting" methodology of one of the world's greatest -- the leopard, and its age-old message, "Do not forget to use your teeth!"

Surviving this incredible economic confusion and mess is going to be about remembering and reverting to what you did, the very first time you did it! How did you find, court and close your very first client? What did your initial market offering that has made you the success you are today look like? Revisit it, and re-acquaint yourself with it. You and your entire organization, whether it be all three of you, or a Fortune 500 with 15,000 employees, are going to have to rediscover your original client closing equipment. This is going to be your way out and forward through this difficult, current economy.

Never forget that it once worked. It built your business and established your nucleus client base. There are elements of it that are, perhaps, no longer relevant, as well as elements that may be antiquated or outdated. However, the fundamental offering contains within it the DNA of your organization's unique, "signature," market differentiator and closing strategies, which are time-tested and have a proven track record. Get hold of these fundamentals, and remember what your corporation did **before** it allowed all this "stuff" to replace them. I am often asked by high level CEO's and VP's of sales what Leopardology™ would tell them they "need" to do to get their sales teams into the **new** "hunt" of our global economy. My answer is entirely counterintuitive, but it is also thousands of years old and time-tested.

In order to get **new**, one has to get **old**! The seeds for the growth of the next generation of **new** super sales teams and managerial leaders lie in wait within the **old,** original seed that put your corporation in business. In a changed "market territory," perhaps with different nuances, leopard are having the same phenomenal success using the same core, original and "award winning" equipment and "closing" techniques in their "market" hunt of 2009 that they did in their "market" hunts of 1985, 1885 and 1785, etc. Going forward, what will change is the condition of their "market place," not, however, the fundamental prospecting and closing methodology that has "naturally" worked for them, and for which they have been built.

The founding principles and behaviors of your organization hold its future. Everyone and everything is shouting out to you, "Adapt or die!" What they should be saying is, "Adapt to your I!" Meaning: Adapt your entire organization, and all its "stuff," to reflect your original market offering, which got you started, and from which you have entirely veered. We receive this "Adapt or die!" communication as a message to throw off our old business ideals for new, current "stuff." This, my friends, will get you killed on your "hunt" for market penetration. "Adapt to your I!" is the call to "adapt" your current market offering to resemble its founding ancestor, which produced great results. It is the call for entrepreneurs and their organizations to get back to doing what they did best, and what they did passionately, when they first did it. Over the next months and years, as the world's economies right themselves, we are going to see a shift and trend away from what we have eloquently mislabeled "diversification." In an effort to survive and thrive, for example, Rolls Royce might consider reclaiming the production of the finest automobiles in the world; Donald Trump might actually get back in the property development business and leave Reality TV to cops; Colgate Corporation might go back into leading the toothpaste industry and leave hand cleansing and disinfectant products to Lysol, etc. There is an extremely thin line between diversification and confusion, and the collective corporate global economy has paid a hefty price learning which is which. The trend is going to pull backwards, not forwards. We will revert to the origin of things -- the known, the tried and the tested. Risking the unknown will become "un-cool." Grass root basement, backyard and garage entrepreneurialism will be in vogue, and Wall Street capitalizations and IPO's will actually be backed by hard assets and current trading performance. Our captains of industry will embrace what has worked, not what might. Venture capital will go to innovative new ideas that enhance the delivery of existing old ones, rather than replacing them. We will use new and exciting technology to deliver original, time-tested and solid market offerings that once closed and kept clients. Corporate think tanks and executive retreats will look to explore what their corporations once did well, and how they did it, before it became buried under all sorts of other "stuff." Banks will actually be in the banking business, not the speculation business. Car manufacturers will actually get back into the business of making safe and reliable cars, rather than competing in the "design awards, even if it does not make sense financially," industry. The individual components of the global economy will start to "hunt **their** hunt."

SOLD - A Four Letter Word
That, At Times, You Shouldn't Use!

In 1999, I attempted to "hunt" a huge jewelry industry giant. Under two hours' drive from Pittsburgh, where I was living at the time, The Sterling Corporation is headquartered in Akron, Ohio. It is a massive, multinational retailer of gold and diamond jewelry with an impressive corporate infrastructure and office. It has several brands in its stable of over 1,400 stores nationwide, including the well-known, free-standing

Jared Jewelers and Sterling Jewelers, as well as Kay Jewelers, located in mall stores throughout the USA. Let me put it to you this way: This "account" is a huge, massive, fully grown 2,500 pound African Buffalo that requires the full power of the lion pride to "close" and is certainly no prospect for a solo, solitary hunter like a leopard! So now, I come along in all my glory and my 1987 Mazda 626, showing about 185,000 miles on the clock. Having been in the USA and in the jewelry industry for two years at this point, I had learned a thing or two about how things are done in America; I had also learned a lot about the expectation of corporate buyers. Things were, thank G-d, going well, and I was building a large network of freestanding, independent, "mom and pop" clients with a sprinkling of multi-store "big boys." One by one, through perseverance and prayer, I was opening accounts and building both my business and my reputation. Because of the close proximity of their head office and their visual presence in Pittsburgh, I had always had my eye on Sterling's, but was well aware of their size vis-à-vis mine. Clearly, I would not have the inventory holding to support an account of that magnitude. My business model was about niche relationships with retail jewelers and their stores, providing them support for loose diamond calls they might have. This is what the industry calls "short term memorandum" or just "memo." In this scenario, a wholesale vendor, such as I, will consign a diamond into a store for seven days or so, giving the retailer an opportunity to work with a stone and present it to a prospective customer without having to purchase it in advance. Should the retailer sell the stone, the vendor will then invoice it to the retailer within the terms of the pre-established vendor account. Should the stone not sell, it will be returned to the vendor. This is a very common and established method of business in the diamond industry, particularly for larger, more expensive goods, which allows retail jewelers to present and sell diamonds without the need to invest in inventory of such diamonds. Because of my 1987 Mazda 626's quick response time, the small size of my organization, and my ability to offer local, same day service, the "memo" business became my niche, and my business offering was positioned to reflect that. I was "hunting my hunt," and, through focus, dedication, perseverance and patience, I was making progress day by day. But, G-d forbid, we human beings should be content with steady and incremental growth. No, we must take giant steps and run towards the allure of things, promises and rewards that are well out of reach, and, many times, detrimental to our financial well-being.

So, being human as I am, I just had to "hunt" the Sterling Corporation. Being "result-centric," always beginning with the end picture, I could clearly see a dedicated employee stationed in my office, established to do nothing else but handle "memo" paperwork, shipping, returns and invoices to the 1,400 -something stores within their stable. I felt that I had what I needed to make the approach. My car would get me there: My business card and materials were extraordinarily impressive and now included my "piece de resistance," a toll-free number! Let me explain. In 1999, in the jewelry industry as in many others, this was the ultimate litmus test of a company's legitimacy. An 800 number, (long before 888 or 877 became toll-free), was the defining psychological signature of an entity's financial stability and magnitude. I mean, you could be a publicly traded company with a capitalization of a billion dollars, but, if you did not have a toll-free number, you were not taken seriously; it was the equivalent of a company website today. At that time, toll-free numbers were expensive and fairly complicated to get, but I found a national paging service that offered a dedicated toll-free service for $29.00 per month. I used this service until they went out of business in 2005, and, according to their regional manager, I was their highest volume account --outside of the Pittsburgh Medical Examiner! (Yeah, it was **me** and the **ME.**)

People think the banking crisis and the bursting of the mortgage bubble created this economic chaos. It was really ATT, Verizon and Comcast, with the introduction of free, long distance telephone packages that did away with the need for toll-free numbers. Without a toll-free number, how do you know if a company is solid?

As you can imagine, there were several loose diamond buyers within the Sterling Corporation head office, and contacting the exact one who handled "short term memo" was an absolute mission. I worked on it for months and eventually made contact with a gentleman by the name of Steven Marowski (not his real name). It was an ongoing and never-ending phone tag game, which lasted weeks. It was only my South

African accent that kept him intrigued long enough for us to actually connect. After combating and surviving tremendous push back and resistance to even consider another diamond vendor, I sold him on seeing me for at least 15 minutes. A date and time was set for us to meet in his Akron, Ohio corporate office.

It was a Wednesday morning in May, and my 15 minutes to meet with Steve was scheduled for 7:15 am -- yeah, like I said, tremendous push back and resistance. I had left Pittsburgh at about 5:15 am, giving me plenty of time, and I arrived at my location with about twenty minutes to spare. It was a beautiful, spring morning, and I was welcomed onto the premises by several geese that occupied the lake in the front of the property. I was feeling bullish and strong, and, as long as he had not seen me getting out of my 1987 Mazda 626, I believed that this was going to be a slam-dunk. I was well-dressed and looked like I was flown in on a private Lear jet, graciously taking time out to do Sterling Corporation a favor and meet with them. This was a no brainer. Yes, they had vendors in place, but who could duplicate my personal signature service and personality? How could they decline the opportunity to deal with me and my whole story? Ok, so my inventory was minuscule relative to what other vendors could offer them. "So what," I thought; I would simply deal with fewer of their stores and ask South Africa to ramp up my inventory in the USA. I just wanted a foot in the door, and I would grow it from there. At around 7:10 am, I made my way up to the reception area.

After I was announced to Steve, he strategically kept me waiting some 30 minutes before he came out to receive me. We sat in a small, but plush meeting room on the third floor of their building, after we had made our way past a slew of employee "prisoners" confined to their cubicles for 8 hours a day. He was polite, but not very warm at all, and really did not say much. You may remember the school of "corporate buyers" we spoke about in an earlier chapter; well, Steve wrote the syllabus. I knew this was a game of "whoever speaks next loses," so I really said very little about diamonds or our diamond business and spoke mostly about South Africa and De Beers. I placed my company folio and marketing materials, (all of which had been handled with my signature cologne scent), in front of him, pointing to our prominently displayed toll-free number. Steve spent some time looking at it and thumbing through the three page brochure. It was impressive, no doubt, and also gave the sense that Kivi International LLC was something that it was not -- namely, a huge multi-million dollar Pittsburgh-based inventory of loose diamonds, with a substantial infrastructure that even included an entire shipping department that closed at 10:00 pm -- and, its own toll-free number!

Steve then looked up at me and asked me what I was really looking for. I waited a moment or two before answering, during which time an imaginary scene from a Seinfeld TV series played out in my mind. While only a few seconds, it was colorful and went like this: "Steve, you are asking me what I am looking for? Wait, you went to school for this job?.... What the hell do you think I am looking for, coming to see you at 7:15am?.... Pizza and fries?..... Moron!...No, I am really looking to rent space in the building, and someone in Pittsburgh told me you are the guy to speak to....Moron!" I snapped back and did the mature, polite thing and answered Steve's question from a business perspective, as it was asked (although my little daydream was more fun).

I said to Steve that I was looking to become a short term memo vendor to Sterling Corporation, specializing in servicing their customers' larger diamond calls and developing personalized service relationships, perhaps starting with just their west Pennsylvania and Ohio stores. Steve listened attentively to what I was saying and then responded as follows:

I will give you 20 stores to put on your books. The deal is that you will place $100,000.00 of loose goods in each store for a 90 day rotation, to be held on hand by the store as an extended memorandum. Sales will be reported every 30 days, and we expect terms of 90 days. You will also be one of 10 vendors authorized to ship "short term memo" for urgent calls by request of the store managers, which, if unsold, will be returned through our head office within 45 days. That's the deal.

Now, what happened next is truly the most astounding part of this little story, and what you are about to read will explain how it made its way into a chapter dedicated to teaching fellow business professionals to "hunt **your** hunt."

I quickly computed the magnitude and two million dollar financial commitment of the deal being offered and replied with the following insane remark: "**Sold!**"

I had not even closed my lips on the letter "d" before I knew that I had just said one of the most stupid and idiotic things I had ever said in my life. Just then, the rest of the imaginary Seinfeld episode began to play out in my head, and it went something like this:

*Sold? Kivi, what the hell planet did you just fall off of? Forget **him**! What school of profoundly dumb did you just graduate from? Kivi, which are you doing first… raiding your kids' piggy banks to fund the two million dollar rotating inventory layout, or selling your 1987 Mazda 626, (which you bought two years ago for $250.00), to cash flow the 90 day terms? Moron!…*

So profound was my stupidity, and so far had I veered from **my** "hunt," that even Steven Marowski, a corporate buyer that had known me for ten minutes remarked, "Sold? Kivi are you sure about that?"

Of course I was not "sold," and of course I was not able to enter into an arrangement of that caliber and magnitude. In an attempt to build my business and to "stare fear in the face," I had crossed over into a massive lion pride hunt, thinking that I would "make a plan," and somehow metamorphose from a solo solitary leopard into a 22 member strong lion pride. Clearly, you see how ridiculous it was for me to even contemplate bringing a client of this caliber on board. But, such is the pull and pressure that we largely place on ourselves to gain client entry and do business at any cost, even when it is not logistically or financially sound business. Leopardology™, is here to communicate that, by "hunting **your** hunt," not only do you actually achieve and succeed within the hunt you do hunt, but you get to stay alive, financially and emotionally, long enough to engage the bigger and better hunt, when it comes. And, it will come!

I looked up at Steve, the corporate loose diamond buyer, and smiled at him, while I shook my head and said, "Steve, you have beautiful geese in the lake...but, no, Steve...I am not "sold." I am a single leopard, not a lion pride." He smiled and responded with, "Uh-Huh...," understanding that I had misspoken, and that I was **not** "sold!"

I stayed in contact with Steve; we spoke from time to time and actually developed a nice friendship. My honesty and transparency with him occasionally got me some small memo call business in two of their Pittsburgh stores. The lesson it got me was priceless!

Hunt **Your** Hunt.

I Don't Do Windows!

This sub-title and its contents are short, because so is the list of times that we can recall actually saying, "Sorry, but no, I cannot do that." So often, the tipping point that heralded the beginning of the end for small businesses and entrepreneurs was their willingness to step into something that was beyond their scope at the time. Saying "yes" is easy; the true grit and brawn of seasoned business professionals is found in their ability to say "no."

We spend so much time in our business development plans articulating what it is we **do**, and how we intend to do it. Perhaps, of more importance, from the standpoint of staying in business, is the ability to articulate exactly what it is we do **not** do. What exact area of our business or service offering is it that we do not provide? It is counterintuitive, because we feel that it is a limitation and a barrier to client entry. However, the precise opposite is true: Not only does it gain respect and acknowledgement from prospective clients as a statement of professionalism, it also serves to define for us and our client what it is we, in fact, do. It also supports the value and price point of what we are offering. Please notice that people who say they can do anything, say they can do so cheaply. Of course you see the correlation: If you pay peanuts, you get monkeys!

Defining your area of expertise and the parameters of your market offering is, perhaps, the single most important thing you can do to ensure the longevity of a business venture. It starts by identifying what it is that you categorically do **not** do. If you do not do windows, don't do them, period! By understanding what your "hunt" is **not**, you will come to a new understanding of what your "hunt" truly **is**!

Hunt **Your** Hunt.

Chapter 12

Keeping What You Kill!

Positive Predatory Pillar™ No. 6

In the bush:

Assess the risk-to-reward ratio and maximize client retention and profit: Accepted as a phenomenon of the natural world, the ability leopard have to hoist their prey 15 - 20 feet up in a tree allows them to feed in peace and to maximize their return.

Making "clients" is one thing: Retaining them for repeat business, safe from competitor predators, is another.

TO WATCH LEOPARD "tree" their prey is truly like watching poetry in motion and is regarded as a phenomenon in zoological science.

The event I am about to share with you was a unique and privileged, once- in-a-lifetime experience that came about entirely coincidentally. I originally wrote this segment without the detailed background to the story, but my wife and my publisher petitioned, insisting that it contained too much of me to withhold from my readers.

In 1987, I had taken three friends, visiting from overseas, into the bush for a four day photo safari in the Kruger National Park in South Africa. We were staying in the very remote and secluded Pafuri Bush Camp in the far north region, only 10 kilometers away from the northern border of South Africa and Mozambique. This area is hardly known, let alone traveled by game-reservers, (South African term used to refer to people who are regular visitors to the bush), who frequent the more popular southern region of the park. It sits in a low rainfall area, is very hot and dry, and is less welcoming to guests than its counterparts in the southern region of the park. At that time, its two camps offered bare minimum amenities, should one need supplies, medical attention or vehicle repair, for example. But, it's the real deal, blistering hot, isolated, slightly volatile and unpredictable wild Africa that, because of the scarcity of water, can offer unusual game and bird viewing opportunities to the trained eye.

Correct, you got it…the Peugeot, all wheel drive vehicle, which we had borrowed from family friends, had broken down, and a game ranger had towed us back to the bush camp. Long story short, we were stuck in the camp, waiting for a Peugeot dealer in Johannesburg to ship a part to the dealer in Nelspruit, who in turn would send the part through to the mechanic in Skakuza. The plan was that the mechanic and the part would then make the 360 kilometer drive up to Pafuri Bush Camp to install this "shifting arm sleeve," or something like that, on this unique clutch mechanism, brought to us compliments of France. Now, strictly because G-d loves me and knows that I am an adrenalin junky for natural adventure and things "slightly" out of the ordinary, I had a chance meeting with an unusual group of individuals, who generated a once-in-a-lifetime experience, a small anecdote of which serves as the basis of this chapter. (If I ever get to it.)

It was in the middle of the day; I had gone to the camp "office" to use the camp radio, the only form of communication at that time, to contact Skakuza and check on the status of things with the mechanic. After about ten minutes, we made contact only to hear, "…nothing yet." As I walked out of the thatched "panduki" (hut) that served as the office in this very remote and unfrequented camp, I saw this 4x4 vehicle pull in past the camp gates. It was an open back pick-up with four heavily armed guys sitting in the back. There were two men in the front cab, and they were pulling an odd looking trailer that appeared to contain liquid. I had a hunch I knew who and what they were, but went over, curious to engage them as they alighted from the vehicle. The dust, their fatigue and their overall condition clearly indicated it had been a long trip. I confirmed my guess that they were a team from the SADF (South African Defense Force) anti-poaching and border crossing unit. Having a definite interest in anti-poaching, African wildlife, survival and Special Operation units (and knowing someone who had served in such a unit), I spent some time with them and even bought them "Sparletta" (soft drinks known by their manufacturer's brand in South Africa). They had come in to replenish water and diesel and to rotate out two of their men.

Now, ladies and gentlemen, here is the thing; these boys are for real! They are not just Rambo counterparts and are really like nothing you can imagine. Allow me to explain: This area of South Africa is situated on the far northeast side of the great Kruger National Park and provides access to and from the Limpopo National Park, located between the borders of South Africa and its neighbor Mozambique. Here, there are hundreds of kilometers of raw African bush and savannah, without an overnight option at a Hilton or Sheraton hotel. In these parts, all the relevant "made in Africa" inherent dangers lie in wait, namely: viable landmines left over from civil wars (In 1993, on safari in this region, my wife and I came across an elephant that had been blown apart by a land mine it had inadvertently stepped on.); active elephant and rhino poachers, still looking to score in the covert north African markets; and desperate individuals, attempting illegal and fabulously dangerous border crossings into South Africa. Beyond these designated "anti-poaching units" that spend months at a time in the bush, patrolling these territories, there are the natural obstacles posed by lion, leopard, hyena, cheetah, crocodile, buffalo, elephant, rhinoceros, hippopotamus and about 15 species of snake and scorpion, whose venom is potentially fatal to humans. (The folks that attempt these border crossings would so welcome the relative "picnic outing" that their Mexican counterparts experience, please believe me; I once met a 27 year old man from Zambia, who lost both his legs during a hippopotamus attack while attempting a crossing.) These four to six man anti-poaching units are commissioned jointly by the South African government and the South African National Parks Board: Their job is to patrol these vast boarder regions, tracking and "neutralizing" game poachers, and "containing" illegals attempting to cross over into South Africa. These are not border patrols that have their hands tied by government bureaucracies. They are there to do a job, which they take very seriously; while they are extremely polite and courteous people, they simply take no prisoners. It's Africa, and they are there to preserve it in its pristine glory -- at all costs. They "hunt" on purpose and achieve results. They told me that they could be out in the bush for four to eight weeks at a time, moving 50 kilometers a day on foot patrols. With the mix of two white men and four black men, the internal bond of trust and life dependence in this unit reflected nothing at all of what outside eyes would anticipate in the land of historical apartheid. Their interaction was seamless, and without the hang-ups we like to project onto cultures different from our own. In fact, this was a microcosm of the real South Africa that contains the thread of mutual respect and appreciation for the knowledge which its different and diverse cultures offer. Each one of these folks was a bastion of survival, tracking and bush knowledge. Each of them intimately understood the rhythm of Africa and its wildlife, because it marched with the beat of their own drum. These units were, and most likely still are, comprised of a precise mix of ancient, tribal, traditional and contemporary tracking and survival expertise, along with the best knowledge and equipment that western culture has to offer. No, no… do not get me wrong; these folks had read "Chapter 11" and fundamentally understood the culture of "traveling light." They did not wear impressive uniforms, pinned lapels, and all sorts of other "stuff" that one would associate with what Hollywood portrays as a Special Operation soldier. They were skeleton light and carried only bare necessities; but, everything they did carry had specific application and purpose. These guys were all hard-core "bossies" (Afrikaans term for bush dwellers). There was nothing extra, no "stuff" -- mental, emotional or physical -- to confuse them about the mission objective at hand; there was nothing to weigh them down, preventing them from nimbly managing change while on the "hunt." (Maybe I should end the chapter right here?)

My friends were waiting for my return with an update, and I had already spent an hour talking with these guys. As I stood up to say goodbye, their unit leader wished me well and said, "Enjoy your afternoon game drive; maybe you will see wild dogs." This part of Kruger is known to have populations of these beautiful predators that are now an endangered species. I thanked him for his wishes, but explained our situation to him, telling him we were waiting on a Peugeot part from Skakuza. The Lieutenant Colonel, whose name I do not remember, (nor would I want to mention because of what follows), looked at me and said to me in Afrikaans, "You will still be waiting when we are back here in a month." I asked him what he meant by that. He answered with certain expletives, (that I do not want my children reading), and explained that I was in the deep bush, where time does not mean what it means in the city. Back then, the Kruger National Park was not the international tourist destination that it currently is, attuned to visitor needs and services. He thought that getting the part to Skakuza would not be the hold-up at all, perhaps a day or two; however, he also thought that getting it up to the most northern point of the park, where we were, and with a mechanic to install it, would take a week or two, if not more -- no joke. He gestured me to come in close and made the following suggestion: He said that he and his team were moving out in the morning and were heading to Skakuza camp for a vehicle swap out and resupply. He recommended that I get to Skakuza, get the part in my hand, find the mechanic and his vehicle, and use the international language of money to "encourage" the mechanic to assist us, sooner rather than later, using the roads outside the park to cut the trip down by 9 hours.

He then looked at me and said in Afrikaans:

Now listen carefully, I can give you a ride to Skakuza with us, but, two things...number one, it never happened... number two, it will take us two days, and we will be in the bush overnight...in places you are not supposed to be.

So, people, of course you understand that I could not refuse an offer like that. It was not the ride to Skakuza; it was the "not supposed to be" part that I could not refuse. I told my friends that "someone" was giving me a ride to Skakuza, that I was bringing the part and a mechanic back up to fix the car, and that I would see them in two to three days. Shalom! The next morning, I was standing at the gate at 4:00 am, two hours before its official opening, but, hey, I was with the army now!

I jumped into the front cab, sat between the unit leader, who was driving, and one of the team members and positioned my legs between several R1 and R4 rifles. This was too good, somewhat stupid, questionably beneficial to our situation, and, I think, illegal from a military rule and regulation standpoint. But, hey, they were just trying to help a stranded tourist. I was sure my parents would not have thought this a good idea, but I also knew that my father would have wanted to hear every detail, and, most likely, would have done the same.

Only speaking Afrikaans, the man I simply call "Lieutenant Colonel" asked me two questions as I got in, and, I quote: "Do you know the bush?" and "Are you a South African?" I proudly answered, "Not as well as you do," and "Yes." He responded by spitting something he was chewing out the window into the pitch black wilderness. I took that as a good sign! We reacquainted ourselves quickly, but basically settled in for the long drive. I was excited about this little adventure and had no idea what I was in for, but, then, neither did they. This clashing of cultures that was now mobile in a 4x4 pick-up, pulling a specialized trailer with drinkable water deep in Africa, now took diversity to a whole new level. These folks did not know Jews exist, let alone an Orthodox "Jungle" Jew such as I, who had to stop to put on phylacteries and attend to morning prayers, but who could also strip and reassemble one of those R4 rifles in 12 seconds. David (obviously his "bush name"), who was a Shangaan tracker and really only spoke Zulu dialects and some Afrikaans, sat on my left at the passenger window, which was all the way down. (Vehicle air conditioning is not good bush etiquette, although my father, who was born in the "ice age," is disagreeing as he reads this. It is not natural and is hard on the engine). It was now about 5:30 am, and all was well. We were traveling on the main road, heading towards Shingwedzi Camp, which was about 110 kilometers south of where we had started. It was mostly uneventful, and we really had not seen much game at all, in spite of the early start. I was not "getting" something here! What would take two days? If we just headed straight on down to Skakuza Camp, we could easily make it by nightfall. I was thinking that Lieutenant Colonel really did have a problem keeping time, not only in the bush, but in general. And, what was up with the "...and we will be in places you are not supposed to be..."? What was the problem here? I was allowed to be on the main road down to Skakuza; ten minutes later, everything changed! Big time!

We suddenly pulled off the road towards the left and onto a gravel patch. Lieutenant Colonel gave a good smack on the horn, generating a loud burst that would awaken anyone, including lion or leopard in the grass nearby. David got out and did an inspection of all the tires and the trailer hitch carrying that ever precious water. The Lieutenant Colonel looked around in a rush and only said to me, "Two minutes." The guys in the back jumped out, stretched and lit up some hand rolled cigarettes, while one used the "facilities." Everyone was back in the truck in minutes. We pulled off, and, so started one of my most memorable deep bush safaris, courtesy of a seriously hard-core anti-poaching unit. We did not rejoin the tar road south to Skakuza, but followed a power line trail with a huge "No Entry" sign posted. We were now heading east towards Mozambique. Now, I got it; we would not be in Skakuza for two days, and I was not supposed to be here.

The tales, with all their twists and turns, from my adventure with these dedicated, beyond hardened soldiers are really the making of another book, (as is the story of how I got a mechanic and a part back up north to repair our Peugeot). And, thank you for bearing with me, thus far, to introduce the point of Leopardology™ that I wanted to illustrate.

So, what is your point, Kivi?

The mission was simple. Lieutenant Colonel was dropping in two new pairs of fresh legs and was switching out a near empty drinking water trailer. The time was now close to noon, and, through a network of badly decayed dirt and drainage roads, only passable in a 4x4, we had arrived at what was evidently a rendezvous point for this unit. We were in the middle of absolutely nowhere, in protected wilderness unavailable to the public! We came up to a location where there was a huge baobab tree that served as a demarcation. A short distance away, anchored to surrounding brush and covered with a military camouflage tarp, was another trailer just like the one we were towing. Beyond that, there was no sign of human life or base camp activity whatsoever.

After switching the trailers out and resupplying fresh drinking water to what I assumed would be the foot patrols, we took time out to relax. A small fire was made, some tea was brewed, some food was had, and I got my chance to attend to my prayers. This was the topic of conversation for the next two or so hours with the remaining men. Thinking that I was a "holy man," they were totally intrigued and thought that I was brought in to help them track the poachers with the spirit of my forefathers. Lieutenant Colonel told me to stay put with two of the guys, while he and David disappeared into the bush. I had seen them prepare to leave by gearing up, (i.e. water and ammunition), and they were out of sight in seconds. I did not ask too many questions, but I learned that they had gone to check on a hide that the unit had built somewhere out there, which apparently overlooked a commonly used poacher route to and from Mozambique. They were expected back within two to three hours. The heat was unreal, and we had shade from a temporary tarp lean-to that came off the truck. The area was fairly thick, bush savannah with mopane and red bushwillow as far as the eye could see. The guys wanted me to stay down low, keeping our position undetected by scouting poachers. I loved every minute of this, hot as it was. I saw lots of general game here and there, but the treat was a sighting of elephant and giraffe well off in the distance. This was definitely viable predator territory, because there was prey to be had. I asked the guys about their safety strategies, particularly regarding lion and leopard. Perhaps, because it was in the heat of the day and not a usual time for predator sightings, they were totally unimpressed with the question and barely understood it. They largely ignored it, but did mention that, soon, they would do a "spoor" (foot print) check on the perimeter of our temporary rest site. This is common bush practice that simply lets you know that, "Oh, by the way…you are right in the middle of a large lion pride that is moving through…," but has little to do with the game plan (if you will excuse the pun), when they do attack. I was certainly with a heavily armed crew, but I was also more exposed than I had ever been in "big five" country. I stayed on or near the truck at all times. While its metal was hot enough to fry an egg, it was off the ground, and I liked the idea that it had several weapons in it.

Once the Lieutenant Colonel and his team member returned, they rested awhile before we moved out again. Soon, there would be three hours of more "bundu bashing" (bush driving), deeper into the soul of Africa, until about a half hour before sunset. Having come up from a partially dry, and sometimes wet, river bed about 300 feet before, we unexpectedly came into a clearing that immediately lead into an area of unusually thick brush and arching trees. I now had only about 15 minutes of daylight left to acquaint myself with the two new faces I met there and with the bush camp hide that served as this unit's central bush camp. There were some mustard trees and several other large trees within 20 feet of the entrance to this bush camp, which also concealed it. Immediately, it occurred to me that the stronger effort here was aimed at keeping this location hidden from people, more so than from animals, and that these poachers must mean serious business. The camp site was a perfect synthesis of traditional bush knowledge and military know-how. There was a fireplace in the middle with a permanently simmering log, and some tarp covered areas on the perimeter of this circular camp site that provided sun and rain shelter. Everything was well organized in the camp; at the same time, there was nothing you couldn't walk away from in five seconds flat. There was an "ablution" area consisting of dried thatch, a hole and a shovel, which was private but did not require you to separate from the group in order to use it. If one did not know how or where to find this bush camp sight, it would not be something one could find alone. The fire was the camp's protector against predators, but one of the guys was, at all times, on watch for poachers. The men in the unit would eat freshly killed meat, but in small amounts that they skinned and carried a fair distance away from the camp to avoid attracting predators. (Carcasses left behind by the unit would become a pleasant find for scavengers like hyena and jackals.) The men were preparing some dinner, which I kindly declined because it was not kosher. I had some fruits and vegetables, but, let me tell you, that impala meat smelled and looked delicious. One of the men shared that his grandfather was the "Umfundisi" (religious man) in his hometown, and that he, too, had to bless the food in his village. When I explained that kosher meat was more involved than that, he insisted that he knew the prayer, and that he could say it on the impala meat rendering it "kosher." Kosher then became the next fascinating discussion with a diverse bunch of hard-core specialists, who think that even having to cook the meat before you eat it is optional.

Lieutenant Colonel called me to the truck and showed me an R4 rifle that was in the cab in a specially designed vertical holder, along with a box of ammo clips. He turned to me, and, once again, asked me two questions, this time pausing for a response between them: "Do you know this weapon?" and "Are you taking malaria tablets?" I answered affirmative to both. He walked over to the fire, took off his shirt, as the others had done, and began to relax by the fire and eat. I then spent much time learning of the magnitude, severity and destruction of the poaching activities in the Kruger Park, as well as around the world. I was educated about the whole chain of command within which these poachers operate, and how, and by whom, they are funded. I began to understand that this was an all out war on these well armed poachers, and that, perhaps, this might have been more stupid than I originally had thought. I figured this was a one-way street, and that we were looking for the bad guys. I was not aware that poachers send out scouts to actively find and engage these anti-poaching units, so as to blow their cover: I did not quite realize that the bad guys were also looking for us. This could get nasty, and I could get caught in a gunfight here between the unit and the poachers, which apparently sometimes happens! How irresponsible and illegal to put a civilian in the middle of this! Lieutenant Colonel could lose his entire career over something like this. Then I remembered, "…it never happened." But, it was when I got my sleeping instruction from the Lieutenant Colonel that the total depth of my stupidity became clear.

It was 9:00 pm and late for the bush; time to turn in. We were leaving at 5:00 am, and, apparently, had one other "stop" to make before coming into Skakuza by 6:00 pm the next day. I was happy to catch some "Z's" anywhere, but my instruction was as follows, and I quote: (translated verbatim from Afrikaans) "Kivi, you will sleep in the front cab of the 4x4; that R4 is on safety, and that magazine is full; there are more mags on the rack box that I showed you before; it is very simple; if you awaken and see people wearing T-shirts, shooting AK47's, or, if you see a buffalo in the camp, shoot that **#$%&** gun as much as you can!; marry that trigger! Understand? (Chuckle)…." I replied with, "I got it!" and then pretended he was joking. But, he was not!

So, it was right about here where my publishers, riveted but confused, politely asked me if I was writing another book, or if I ever intended to bring my readers back to Leopardology™, and the title of this chapter, "Keeping What You Kill"? I apologized, stating that they were entirely correct and went on to write the following:

When I eventually put my head down to get some sleep, I was so exhausted that I did not think much about the not so clever thing I had done. Besides, I was living my dream. The mosquitoes were vicious, but I had a Tabard repellant stick, which I plastered all over myself. The night sounds were symphonic, and I fell into a deep sleep. The night was, thank G-d, uneventful -- no buffalo and no men in T-shirts with AK47's. I was so gone that I would not have heard them anyway, but I certainly did hear the tapping on the cab roof that awakened me. It was 4:30 am; I was disorientated and had to actively remember my stupidity in order to remember where I was.

Now here it is folks! As soon as I opened the door of the 4x4, I could smell it. Immediately, and in a whisper, Lieutenant Colonel said to me, "Passop (be careful), something has made a kill overnight right by our camp." It was a pungent, but fresh, kill smell; it was that distinct "guts" smell of intestines and bowel that anyone who has ever dissected anything knows all about. The air was thick with the sounds of pre-dawn Africa and that indigenous tension between the hunter and the hunted. I had smelled kills several times before, but this was a distinct, "just happened now" smell that had not, yet, had the time to "mature" and develop a nose bouquet like a fine wine. We could also smell its closeness. I know that sounds strange, but there was that freshly dead "flesh-bones-blood-body-parts" "scent" that you can only pick up when you are really close to it. One of the men gave a general instruction to be very quiet while packing to move out, because, he said, "That leopard may have cubs." I thought to myself, "How the heck does he know that it was a leopard kill?... It could be anything!" I quickly remembered that the men rotate around the clock on watch and would have heard the noisy commotion of a lion pride, hyena or wild dog pack.

Mazal Tov, and here is the teaching point! As we moved out, leaving three others behind to begin foot patrols, it was not 20 feet from the bush camp entrance, up in a "V" limb of one of those big trees, that we saw the leopard with its still warm and disemboweled baby zebra "client." Lieutenant Colonel stopped for a moment, allowing me to take this in. We watched for a while as he shined a military issue mag-light torch between the leopard in the tree and the entrails it had disemboweled and left on the ground. This is what smelled so bad, but I knew I was witnessing and smelling life in the raw. He and David had a discussion in Zulu confirming that this was a dominant territorial male leopard they knew from the riverbed a few kilos behind us.

Hyena...Love Your Guts!

Of course it was a leopard! What else could use such stealth, such silence, such agility and such strength to "close, sign and hold" a "client" for maximum profit taking, and do so entirely undetected. It was the silence and the precision of this leopard's "transaction" that was blowing me away. I could not believe that I had spent the night not 25 feet away from where an entire "client holding" event was taking place in absolute silence. So polished, finessed and instinctive is a leopard's ability to identify, manage and execute a holding environment way up in a tree, that we had only the early morning "aromas" to alert us to the fact that a substantial "client" event had occurred. Sometimes leopard bury what they disembowel from their "client," sometimes they don't. But, by disemboweling the zebra, a leopard does two ingenious things: Firstly, it lightens the carcass, making it that much easier to hoist and position in the tree, while, at the same time, allowing it to last longer before rotting; Secondly, it leaves some minor "profit" below for its competitors. Beyond the fact that it gets rid of the main scent trail from a dead carcass, this is an astonishing instinct that allows its competitors, like hyena, who **will** be there in moments, to be busy with something other than trying to steal its hard earned "client."

This is a key psychological component of Leopardology™. Leopard behave out of **instinctive abundance**; we human beings have to choose to do so. Transact and trade from a place of abundance. To take large clients and profit, one has to be willing to literally and figuratively "feed" others, even one's competitors. It is not only good for the health of the "market" in general, but it helps build symbiotic relationships. Take a look at this: The hyenas that now find or dig up the zebra entrails and eat them get rid of the main scent trail that will potentially lead lion to the leopard's kill. Trade from a place of abundance; it will build your business. There is a sentiment, particularly among young entrepreneurs, that, unless a venture or market initiative totally consumes market share and eliminates competition, it is not so viable. I believe this comes from **negative** predatory business thinking and is clearly not a natural instinct, as this element of Leopardology™ illustrates. Critically understanding that things, including competitors, are designed to work symbiotically and synergistically with each other will further one's business growth much more than attempting to "kill" the competition. Your competitors' well-being is a sign of life for your well-being. It has worked this way in the natural world for thousands of years and is obviously successful.

Don't...Get Down From There.

The African leopard has a remarkable ability to hoist its prey, perhaps twice its own body weight, 15, 20 or even 30 feet up into the limb structures of an appropriate tree for maximum "profit" taking. This is the incredible opus of the leopard's hunt, "client retention!" Once its "client" is firmly secured in its holding environment, the leopard will enjoy the full reward of its hunting effort and maximize its return on energy and risk investment. Safe from other predators and the prospect of losing its "client" to hungry competitors, this leopard will now slowly and completely "take profit." This, then, serves as a pristine holding and retention environment, where both the leopard and its cubs can feed on their "client" without pressure or concern.

The process, however, began long before the hunt ever did. Included in the leopard's commitment to study its hunting territory (Positive Predatory Pillar No. 2; Chapters 4 and 5) is a disciplined dedication to identifying viable holding environments to receive its "client" post-hunt. This dedication is a fundamental aspect of the success of the leopard's hunt. When it is not hunting, it is taking inventory of, and demarcating, appropriate trees that will serve this purpose. Multiple factors, such as its weight bearing capacity, its access, its tree line and branch cover, its overall strength, etc., are considered and noted. Clearly, the time to consider a holding environment is not when you urgently need it. Rather, this aspect of the leopard's hunt is well in place and on tap before the hunt ever occurs. Immediately, subsequent to a successful hunt, leopard will instinctively access their data bank of holding environment options and flawlessly implement a decision based on those options.

It is not only the incredible display of strength and agility it takes to execute this feat that is remarkable; it is also the degree to which this is so instinctive within the African leopard, almost from birth. As we have discussed, leopard are equipped with permanently exposed drew claws and very wide paws because of the time they spend in trees. They are instinctively tree climbers and have been given specific tooling for this function. Before cubs learn anything about hunting, they must master tree climbing and extraordinary dexterity in the tree. This is so, because, as solo, solitary hunters, the success of their hunt largely depends on their ability to hold onto their kill. The tree, their knowledge of it, and their ability to climb and maneuver within it, is the ultimate determinant of whether or not they eat and survive. Once out of their den, cubs spend the majority of the next four to six months exploring every branch, limb and cluster of the trees around them. It is their "client" holding environment, and they need to know it intimately. Let me ask you a question, if I may. Do you know where the electrical control panel is in your office?

Eat Slowly And Chew!

This has to be one of the least available luxuries afforded any predator in the wild, but for one; you got it, the African leopard. Allow me to explain: Much as it is in the "jungle" of commerce, the most vulnerable moment of any hunt initiative, beyond the "close" itself, is the time that immediately follows a successful closure. All of them -- lion, leopard, cheetah, hyena, etc. -- are extremely vulnerable to each other, moments after a kill has taken place. However, leopard do something about that and dramatically diminish their risk of attack, greatly increasing their "client retention" rate and ultimate success as a species. Let's flesh this out, if you will excuse the pun: The chances are strong that a competitor predator has either been alerted to a hunt by the noise and commotion, or by the tell-tale signs that give it up (i.e. vultures circling above, or apex scavengers, like black backed jackal, aardwolf and spotted hyena scurrying intently in a certain direction, etc.). As such, "keeping your kill" in the bush is an extremely important and critical component of success. Sound familiar? Sure it does, because in our world of commerce, the same is true. You can sell and close all day long, but if you cannot "keep your client" and you lose it to competitors, you will not eat, let alone take profit! The large lion prides rely on their huge power and numbers to fend off smaller, nagging competitors. Smaller, less powerful conglomerates, like cheetah pairs or trios, must waste no time at all; they must quickly, messily and inefficiently start eating what they can, knowing that, at any time, their "client" can be appropriated. And, then, there is our leopard. As a solo, solitary hunter, aware of both its strengths and its weaknesses, it refuses to play the field and expose itself to the risk of losing its "client." So, immediately after "closing" its "client," it takes its kill into a holding environment, securing and procuring it for total "client" retention and engagement. It will feed completely and fully, and, so will its cubs. It will, quite literally, eat slowly and chew its food, maximizing the nutritional value of its "client," taking total "profit."

Chapter 13

The Art of Keeping Clients & Profits!

Positive Predatory Pillar ™ No. 6

In the boardroom:

Assess the risk-to-reward ratio and maximize client retention and profit: Accepted as a phenomenon of the natural world, the ability leopard have to hoist their prey 15 - 20 feet up in a tree allows them to feed in peace and to maximize their return.

Making "clients" is one thing: Retaining them for repeat business, safe from competitor predators, is another.

DO NOT TAKE my word for it. Examine your own experience and that of business people you know and trust. The sweet spot and tipping point of successful business is a thing called the "repeat client" and the consequent transaction that reflects the successful transfer and confirmation of trust, honesty and integrity purveyed on the first encounter. It is the strongest possible affirmation that a client can make regarding his willingness to transact with you and to expand the business relationship further. Repeat business is a nonverbal communication from a client telling you that the most difficult aspect of client entry is over and has been successful. From here on out, your relationship will be about service, maintenance and client retention. The "hunt" is over; you must now keep your "client" from competitors.

Particularly in an economic slump, (polite word for collapse), such as the current global market condition, doing repeat and expanded business with existing clients is so much easier, safer and cost-effective than risking new client "hunts." However, client retention is, perhaps, one of the least understood and least addressed components in the contemporary "MBA" corporate mindset. Businesses attend to client retention in very much the same way that they attend to 401K plans. Meaning, it is largely seen as a function that someone on an internal HR team is responsible for implementing and managing. It is an operating function that needs to fall under someone's specific job description and responsibility; someone needs to "take care of it and do it." And, if we don't have someone who does it, we will either hire someone or contract it out to a company that can do it for us. In the hallways and walls of corporations and organizations the world over, attending to "client retention" often sounds like this:

Ok, we need to show client appreciation and have our customers understand that we value their patronage and business. Here is what we need to do. We'll take the Yellow Pages and find one of those corporate gift vendors that prints logos and stuff on all sorts of junk. You know, one of those companies that does all that "junk" that **we** *are always getting from* **our** *vendors. We'll go through the catalog and choose something nice, like a set of personalized golf balls, a year planner or a gym bag, and stick our company logo on it with a message: "We appreciate you," signed, our chairman. Oh, and order in bulk to save money. Let's get on it and get them out to our client base before Christmas, please.*

I know you are laughing, because you have either given that little speech or received it, right? (And, by the way, I have a good friend in that business, so please support it!)

Leopardology™ is here to introduce a paradigm shift, which suggests that client retention is not something you can implement, manage or buy. It is, in fact, an art, and, very much like the leopard's "treeing" ability, "poetry in motion," when well performed. For those entrepreneurs, business managers and CEO's who have identified this as such, huge rewards have been reaped. (I am a firm believer that, while it is true that nothing is free in this world, it is also true that no positive effort goes without reward.) For this select group of entrepreneurs, tremendous time, effort, energy and expense are invested in developing and refining this art form. Their sweet and abundant payoff comes in the form of client retention; this produces maximization of client profit and regular repeat business that often eludes their competitors.

In a market recession, or even depression, it is this that allows them to survive the dip and be there for the upturn. In a booming market, it is the thing that allows them to keep what they have "hunted" away from the well financed and resourced competition.

Understanding, developing and investing in personal and organizational client retention skills is, perhaps, one of the most significant endeavors an entrepreneur can pursue in starting a new business -- or surviving in an existing one.

Experiential Selling...The New Relationship Selling!

...Tony, I want you to meet Kivi from Kivi International. He is a loose diamond vendor based in Pittsburgh (at the time). Forget about relationship selling; dealing with this guy is an entire experience! When you become a client, you will get to go on a virtual safari every time you get your monthly statement!

This is how I was introduced to a fine retail jeweler from Ohio, who went on to become a very good client of ours. Let me back up here: There is no better client than a client-referred client. It simply eliminates much of the risk of the "hunt." Several years ago, I was in a client's store, when a friend of his from out of state, himself a retail jeweler, walked in. My client quickly introduced me to this gentleman with the very kind preamble above. It was at that point that I knew that a conscious and disciplined commitment I had made a year or two before had paid off -- big time. Years ago, it was very common and popular in the jewelry industry for vendors to send out monthly newsletters to their clients. These were industry updates and obviously were intended as branding and client retention opportunities for the vendors. Being on several competitor vendors' lists as a client, I would receive quite a few of these every month. While they were informational and sometimes technical, they were all the same. In fact, at one point, there was one template being produced by a third party that was compiling the monthly newsletter and selling it to various vendors. Right there is where I saw a distinct and unique opening for a very specific client retention opportunity. I had an insight into relationship selling that would greatly enhance my business and change my understanding of relationships in general. It would take work and effort, but it would yield very particular client retention results.

These newsletters were supposed to be an individual expression of relationship trading, evident of unique trust relationships that had been built between a particular retail jeweler and a particular wholesale vendor. In seeing the mass distribution of these "special client newsletters," I learned a critical thing about "hunting" clients. It occurred to me that these industry newsletters, themselves, had fallen prey to the "commoditization" of business relationships, and that they reflected a general business trend. Follow me here! Personalized, client oriented "relationship selling" had, itself, become a mass-produced commodity of sale. Insane, right? This is a new but aggressive virus in the "computer" economy we trade in. From a computer with internet access, almost anything and everything can be mass-produced, distributed and "commoditized" faster and cheaper than ever before in history, including the previously un-touchable "relationship selling." Think about it, and call it what you want, but consider, for example, that: eHarmony.com is the mass "commoditization" of interpersonal relationships; Facebook is where this happens for social relationships; and, sites like Plaxo and LinkedIn are where it happens for selling relationships. Society has commercialized the last surviving frontier in the realm of "private" and "exclusive" that humanity had not, until now, yet sacrificed to the powerful dollar bill. Relationship, by very definition, is inherently not mass-producible. And, so, I ask you; how exactly does one have a "relationship" with 1,874 people on one's virtual cyber "wall"? Think about this some more! Relationship -- the very thing that was given to man to define his unique, indispensable and irreplaceable connection with G-d, has, with the click of a button, become common, nonessential and replaceable!

Forget about saving the whale! As a lone crusader, and in my own small, insignificant way, I had to do something about this and save "relationship selling" from commercialism. So, I embarked on something I called "Experiential Selling." I made a commitment to myself and to my small business that every single interaction and contact with a client, verbal or nonverbal, would be a "Kivi" experience that transcends the client relationship "check list" society has mass-produced. I did not want strong selling relationships with my clients. I wanted unexplainable, illogical and almost irrational loyalty and business relationships that were the result of the **experience** it was to transact with me and my company. **Experiential selling** -- that was my focus and passion. I would be fully present and engaged in every client contact, which was also to contain an exclusive and unique dimension of me and my background that was not duplicative. No telephone call took place without the full extent of my South African accent, a story about a witch doctor, a charging lion or men I had known selling blood diamonds in Sierra Leone. No fax communication went out without a second accompanying page offering a picture of a diamond cutter in South Africa, a De Beers mining operation or an anecdotal story of Bushmen in the Kalahari Desert. No meeting took place without my bringing a small, but tangible, trail of South Africa, my family, my home, my people and my country. No order was placed with a catalog company that prints logos on all sorts of stuff. New Years, birthday, anniversary gifts and cards were all hints of the Kivi International experience -- warthog tusk cork screws, wildlife calendars from South Africa, dried elephant dung paper made by villagers in Malawi, Africa (you read that correctly). And, yes, our company newsletter, which accompanied every account statement, was an exclusive virtual safari compiled from my own collection of photographs taken over the years. Entitled "From Factory To Finger," it offered industry news presented from the mines and factories in South Africa. Huge amounts of work went into the production of this newsletter, and I remind you that this preceded the user-friendly desk top publishing software that we have at our disposal today. The newsletter was a huge hit and delivered a "piece" of me with every month's account statement. It often circulated well beyond the store owner or bookkeeper. Regularly, I walked into jewelry stores to comments by sales associates and support staff about safari pictures, or other details. For years, people suggested that I even write a book!

Here is the thing, though. It was not a "newsletter"; rather, it was part and parcel of a total holding environment that allowed me to retain my client and maximize profit. Dealing with my company was an entire cultural and social experience. Business, and some significant business, got done in between the spaces from one experience to the next. I finessed and tweaked my holding environment for each client based on my "Study Your Client" intelligence gathering. With one client, I would talk motor biking in South Africa; with another, it would be the wine farms of Stellenbosch in the Cape; and, with another, it would be about growing up in apartheid South Africa. But, it was always a noncommercialized offering of me and of the specific human being I am.

Client retention begins by identifying the unique and exclusive offering **your** entrepreneurial enterprise or corporation offers the marketplace. Your holding environment, where you will retain your client for maximum profit, is defined by any and all client contact you have. Every form and mode of client contact is a method of delivery for the essence of you and your entity. Your holding environment does not campaign for your clients to deal with you; rather, it reminds them of why they do. If you are consistent and leave no stone unturned, you will successfully engage your clients in "experiential selling" and retain them in a truly unique holding environment. This offers you not only client retention from constantly prowling competitors, but also something we call -- relationship.

Pepsi ....And Coke.

Creating an appropriate holding environment for your clients is an extensive and time-consuming endeavor. It moves well beyond ensuring that there is both Pepsi and Coca Cola in the mini bar, that there is a mirror in the ladies' room, and that you have dedicated client parking available.

It is beyond having an outside contractor attend to your plants and landscaping. This is all-important and crucial to the general health and condition of your "tree." However, to absorb the essence of this critical component of Leopardology™, it is necessary to understand this: A true client holding environment is an all-encompassing commitment to the total, overall physical, as well as mental, offering of your office or store space; it is about creating perfect synergy between the physical space of your environment and the emotional aspects of your market offering.

For instance, do nothing more than just placing your corporate mission statement on the wall of the reception area, and you will have communicated what your business does, but not at all what it feels like. Yes, your holding environment needs to communicate well beyond what you do. In order to fully retain clients for total profit and repeat business, they must get an immediate sense of what your business feels like. Here is the thing. There are, most likely, plenty of people who do what you do. There are likely other businesses that do what yours does. But, none of them **feel** like you or your business. Your offering **feel** is your market differentiator, because it is you. That specific sense and emotive hunch you get when stepping into people's homes or business environments must be instantaneously perceived in your client holding environment. The walls, the floors, the nonverbal and the verbal of everyone concerned must come together to immediately broadcast what your market offering is and what it feels like to transact with it. This is your "tree" from top to bottom. This "tree" is going to hold your precious client in which you have invested and risked much to "hunt."

Abundant Profit…Throw Your Competitors A Bone!

In 1993, still living in Johannesburg, South Africa, I had traveled to Antwerp, Belgium on business. During my four day stay, I had the privilege of a chance meeting with a highly successful, world renowned "diamondteer" and doyen of the diamond industry.

Just for the chance to learn and hear his story, I asked if I could buy him a morning coffee and some breakfast. Because of his "abundant profit" mentality, he warmly accepted and gave me his time. We met early and spent an hour together. It was fascinating and intriguing to hear his journey, first hand. I asked him how he got started in the business, knowing that he came from extremely humble beginnings, but also knowing that the diamond business is an extraordinarily difficult business to break into from the outside. (This has subsequently changed, but so has the diamond business.) He told me something that I have never forgotten, and that has become a life approach for me and my family. He shared with me that, three months after entering the diamond business some 35 years prior, as a broker offering small parcels of goods from one dealer to another, he had an unusual experience. One of his regular vendors had bought a very large parcel of specific loose diamonds that included categories of both colored and colorless polished diamonds. This was a substantial parcel and was certainly the largest, in terms of value, that he, the "diamondteer", had dealt with. A substantial commission could be made brokering this business, but, because of the nature of this very specific parcel, the diamonds really had to be examined in person and at some length by a prospective buyer. This made the parcel very difficult to broker, particularly by someone who was still an unknown entity to the vendor. For this size and caliber business, the buyer and seller really needed undisturbed access to each other. Because of the dollar value of the parcel and the seller's unwillingness to have the goods leave his office, the broker was unable to physically show the diamonds to prospective buyers. He tried brokering the deal on paper, but was unsuccessful due to the nature of this parcel. He told me that he had a real dilemma: The parcel of diamonds was an extremely lucrative buy, and he believed he knew an appropriate buyer who would greatly appreciate the deal, but his hands were tied. He was unable to set up a brokerage situation and was at a stalemate. Needing to feed his young family and hungry for business, he was just confounded by how to put the buyer and seller together, while still earning a commission. So anguished by this, he could not sleep.

While the buyer and seller might keep him "covered" on this particular deal, what would it do to future business? Now that they were aware of each other, where would it leave him as a middleman broker? This incredibly polished gentleman, exuding age-old wisdom and knowledge, sat up and looked me in the eyes. He said to me that he had asked his wife's advice, and she had told him to approach the buyer and communicate to him that, having the buyer's best interest in mind, he was going to place the buyer in direct contact with the seller. His wife had told him to explain that the parcel of diamonds was just too good to pass up, and that, just because he, as broker, might not benefit, he did not want his valued client to miss this profit opportunity. He did just as his wife had advised.

The seller and the buyer did, in fact, meet and spent much time together working out a deal. They did transact directly. The seller paid a finder's commission of a few percentage points to my new friend, the "diamondteer." The buyer, however, did not do the same and was silent for about four weeks, at which point he requested that the broker come to see him in his office. When the "diamondteer" met with the buyer of that large and profitable parcel of diamonds, the buyer said to him the following:

Anyone who considers my well-being as part of his well-being is someone I want to do business with. So, I am not going to pay you a finder's commission like the seller did. I know you cannot get credit and buy your own diamonds. Therefore, I am going to give you back the entire parcel, which I have re-sorted and certified, and we will split the profit. I am now your partner in this parcel and hope to do the same with many more...Mazal!

As he got up from the coffee table to shake my hand, he said "And, that is how I got into the diamond business...I listened to my wife and acted in an abundant way...I, in turn, have put many people into the diamond business the same way..."

Leopard, in an instinctive abundant behavior will allow a bone or two to fall from the tree that serves as their client holding environment. This abundant behavior has symbiotic benefit but is not what generates this conduct. For instance: Hungry and persistent hyena, below, eagerly await these fallen scraps. In so doing, they keep other larger and smaller competitors away from the "holding environment." (Remember, creatures of habit prefer the path of least resistance. A honey badger, African wildcat, or even a pair of lionesses is unlikely to attempt the already dangerous tree climb to rob the leopard of his "client," if several hyena can be found at the base of that tree.) As mentioned earlier, hyena are also ready and willing to clean up the smelly entrails that a leopard has disemboweled before treeing his "client."

This instinctive abundance is a fundament of Leopardolgy TM; it is about adopting a deeper understanding of the very essence of abundance and how it manifests in the natural world.

Warning!! Grab another cup of strong coffee before you read further:

Abundance in "**Nature-Nomics101**" has a slightly different twist from society's version. Here is the deal, quite literally. It is not merely symbiotic in that, if you serve and benefit others, then, in turn, others will serve and benefit you. Rather, it transcends that and is really part of an entire understanding of the synthesis and interconnectedness of the world. It is a comprehensive consciousness that one's function as a human being is to be abundant and giving, not because it benefits one, but because that is the way G-d designed the world and one's involvement in it. In other words, as I pursue my own success as a human being, my abundant thinking and behavior is not a strategy or approach I choose to take in order to succeed; rather, choosing abundance is a manifestation of my humanity and integral to my success as a human being. I act abundantly, because, I am choosing to be all a human being can be. Leopardology™ suggests that the same is so with regards our ability to be abundant and symbiotic with our pursuit of success in the marketplace. The natural DNA of success dictates that it must be abundant and have relevance to others. If it does not, it will not have **longevity, blessing or happiness**. This is a law of the natural world and cannot be broken. Please feel free to ask so many of those before you in the annals of history, (or in the headlines this morning), who have attempted to challenge this premise.

Abundance, whether it be in one's familial life, communal life or professional life, is not just a good idea and clever approach to be learned from the African leopard. No, not at all! It is a fundamental truth and cornerstone of all existence that holds within it the very secret to success, as taught to us by the instinctive behavior of the African leopard.

The "Tree" Between Your Ears...Water It!

For an entrepreneur, business leader and manager of ideas and people, there exists a holding environment that moves beyond your home, community and office. It is not the place or space where you retain your clients for profit and repeat business: It is not your physical counterpart to the tree that the leopard uses to "hold" its "client." Rather, it is the place and space that holds and nourishes the energy, creativity, originality and purity of all that you are and do. It is called your brain. That relatively small space between your ears is the holding environment for all your thoughts, ideas, initiatives and ultimately actions. Your brain is the "tree" where your subconscious and conscious thinking hold and retain your ideas for maximum profit and repeat use. Think about this: Your brain is the holding environment that is responsible for retaining the very essence of your life offering. It is the thing that determines who you will be, what you will say and what you will do.

Corporations spend tens of thousands of dollars employing services and products to keep viruses off their networks and off the computers that hold their valuable client details, market offerings and creative ideas. We leave our offices to go home, or out, where we then indulge in entirely polluting our most critical and pristine holding environment, our brain -- the environment that is entirely responsible for holding all those good ideas, initiatives and strategies that we action the very next morning back in the office.

It is uncomfortable, but prudent, to really examine exactly what it is we are allowing ourselves to be exposed to. What is it that we are allowing to penetrate into that pristine holding environment of our ideas and thoughts? What am I allowing my eyes to see, my ears to hear and my mind to absorb? What books, movies and music am I renting free space in my holding environment? If one is serious about retention and maximizing profits, then it surely starts with the profit taking of one's very own thoughts and ideas! And, how are those ideas and thoughts being influenced by negative or damaging outside input? When your brain does trickle your idea or initiative down to you, in what condition have you received it? Is it pure, pristine and fresh? Leopard like to eat fresh meat; It maximizes risk-to-reward with regards nutrition. Also, eating fresh meat ensures leopard the longest possible "client relationship" before the carcass rots. As entrepreneurs with an unquenchable thirst for truth, efficiency and efficacy, it behooves us to ask ourselves, "Just how 'fresh' are the thoughts and ideas **we** are consuming?"

The government talks about "toxic debt," something you and I can do little about. But, what of "**toxic influence**" that we voluntarily expose ourselves to and can change? I know! There is tremendous societal and peer pressure to embrace much of this toxic influence.

And, clearly, one has to muster tremendous self-confidence and strength to say "No" and refuse to allow the pollution of one's head space. But, my dear readers, please allow me to share with you that doing so will be one of your sweetest victories ever won. Gaining total control and management of what goes into your head will allow you to create a pristine and pure holding environment for the very things that will determine your success -- your thoughts. Additionally, this thought holding environment between your ears that you will have created will also prove to be the only environment that will allow you total control. Your office, store, warehouse or factory is subject to terms and conditions of lease or purchase, etc. There are ordinances, regulations and laws that must be adhered to and that impact what you can or cannot do with a space.

But friends, your head space is entirely yours, and, even as you read these words, there are people fighting for your freedom to keep it that way. You are constitutionally guaranteed the right to be the sole determinant of what enters this sacred space, and whether or not that entry is given a permanent home. No **one**, no **thing**, no "**ism**" and no "**ology**" can strip you of this inalienable right that you have to keep your thought-holding-environment free of negative and toxic contamination. If nothing else, it is my fervent hope and prayer that, this, you have learned from Leopard**ology**™ (How ironic is that?!)

Chapter 14

In "Closing"!

FOR THE AFRICAN leopard, hunting and "closing" prey opportunities on the African savannah and its bush lands is the result of instinctive and intrinsic behavior that is unapologetically handed down from one generation to the next. Leopard exhibit no shame or embarrassment in being known as Africa's most successful predator, and, perhaps, even one of the most efficient and effective "closers" walking the earth. They wear this title regally, literally holding their heads high. They are not uncomfortable with the attention it draws to them, because they are not aware that there is an alternative to their tremendous success. Their success as hunters, "closers," and "retainers" of "clients" and their "profits" is simply who they are and what they do. Leopard are happy because they are unaware of an alternative!

We human beings, on the other hand, are blessed with intelligence, which often we use to fight instinct. However our specific opportunity is to use intelligence to delineate, to decide and to choose. When we decline to engage this process, we become unconscious consumers, having foregone our privilege to choose. We are choosers in life, not passive bystanders. We do not have the liberty and freedom of ignorance; as a result, we are quite aware of failure as a common and regular possibility. We have to choose to focus on and maintain thoughts of success, positivity, efficacy and efficiency. This certainly is not instinctive within us and must be consciously selected from a list of alternative thoughts. When we finally do get hold of our eligibility and viability for success, unlike leopard, we instinctively begin to apologize for it in all sorts of complicated and complex ways.

To be happy, content and satisfied with our success in a particular area, leadership initiative, or business venture, is something we have to choose. Here is why? As human beings, we are aware of the alternative, and that knowledge immediately demands that we choose one thing over another.

And so, my fellow citizens of the world, happiness, the thing we humans "hunt" most of all, is something we choose. It cannot be bought; it cannot be inherited; it cannot be acquired from a book.

It has certainly not been my intention in this book to "tell" you, as a reader, "how" you can achieve success, happiness, etc. I cannot tell you that; nor can anyone else. It is something you choose, not something that chooses you. My sole and humble intent in sharing **Leopardology**™ with readers around the world is this: I wish to share with others the simple and basic business strategies and marketing initiatives that allowed me to build my business in a foreign country, nine thousand miles away from everything I knew and cherished. Even more so, it is my passionate desire to infuse others with the very same powerful and seminal message of self that it came to give me at a time of tremendous challenge.

As this book goes to press, the world around us, religiously, socially, politically, financially and communally is truly dark and confusing. We are all searching, not only for the key to survival, but for the opportunity that lies **beyond survival**. We are, right now, in search of our tomorrows -- not only ours, but those of our children and grandchildren. While I am not able to articulate what tomorrow will be or what it will look like, I can tell you this: It will be abundant, and it will involve you in your very essence, in your perfection, the way G-d created you.

In "closing," please allow me to offer the following: I so gratefully and humbly thank you for indulging me by reading this book and sharing your time with me. As we all engage in our own "hunt" for success, let us know, viscerally and soulfully, that we are tooled and equipped with what it takes to succeed. Let us know that we have what we need to succeed, and that, what we do not have, we do not need. Let us know that our happiness and joy lie in our choosing to acknowledge the pristine and precise human beings we are, not in the ones we think we should be. Let us know that our happiness, and, in turn, our success, lie in our identifying our particular and specific tooling, apparatus and equipment and committing entirely to deploying it on our "hunt" for success!

May G-d bless you to live your life not as an unconscious **consumer**, but as a conscious **chooser.**

About the author

Born in Johannesburg, South Africa, Kivi Bernhard lived and breathed the African bush until the age of 29, when he relocated to the United States of America. In 1997, he arrived on the shores of America with his wife, their four daughters and thirteen pieces of luggage. In his pocket was a check for $860.22, which constituted his entire net worth, and which was to serve as the founding capital for Kivi International LLC, a loose diamond, wholesale and distribution business that would grow to serve major fine retail jewelers and dealers, both nationally and internationally. Although Kivi's parents, themselves, were American citizens, who had emigrated to South Africa in 1964, Kivi was born to the soil of Africa, and, at a very early age, developed keen observation skills and a passion for Africa's wildlife.

As Kivi grew and developed his diamond business, he would use the memories and knowledge of those finessed predators of Africa, those incredible hunters and "closers," to inform, motivate and inspire him to persevere. By studying and analyzing the hunting habits of Africa's most successful predator, the African leopard, Kivi developed a style of business thinking, which he called **Leopardology**™. This is critical and fundamental business thinking and strategy gleaned from the hunt of the African leopard. Having been blessed with the "gift of gab," Kivi was often asked to share his ideas at jewelry industry events, and, over time, developed his first business keynote entitled: The Hunt For Success – Critical Business Thinking From Africa's Most Successful Predator! The keynote was a huge success with audience members and meeting planners alike, and was a synthesis of the business journey Kivi had traveled in America and his love and passion for Africa and its wildlife.

Over time, Kivi Bernhard has emerged as one of the most dynamic, original and gifted professional keynote speakers in the world today, sought after by leading speaker bureaus and meeting planners. From 6000 member audiences of Fortune 500 companies to exclusive ten member CEO think tanks, Kivi Bernhard has engaged audiences around the world and continues to be recognized for the creativity, richness and relevance of Leopardology™. Beyond the award-winning video footage, which includes scenes of predatory behavior never before caught on film, Kivi Bernhard's keynotes are delivered with a platform presence and excellence that fellow colleagues at the National Speakers Association only refer to as "masterful".

Kivi Bernhard currently lives in Atlanta, Georgia with his ever patient and loving wife and daughters.

The offering of this book to the marketplace has been the fulfillment of a lifetime goal for Kivi. Through podcasts, newsletters, social media, speaking engagements and various media outlets, Kivi Bernhard intends to stay connected to his readers and audience members and encourages them to make use of the contact information below. Oh – and keep checking his website for details about an exclusive, luxurious four day **Leopardology™ Safari** deep in the beautiful bush of South Africa. (Did we mention one lucky person will travel free?)

KIVI BERNHARD INTERNATIONAL

2897 North Druid Hills Rd.

Suite No. 273

Atlanta, GA 30329

Tel: 404.832.8250

Fax: 404.228.3254

Email: Kivi@KiviBernhard.com

Website: www.KIVIBERNHARD.com

BUY A SHARE OF THE FUTURE IN YOUR COMMUNITY

These certificates make great holiday, graduation and birthday gifts that can be personalized with the recipient's name. The cost of one S.H.A.R.E. or one square foot is $54.17. The personalized certificate is suitable for framing and will state the number of shares purchased and the amount of each share, as well as the recipient's name. The home that you participate in "building" will last for many years and will continue to grow in value.

Here is a sample SHARE certificate:

HABITAT FOR HUMANITY

THIS CERTIFIES THAT

YOUR NAME HERE

HAS INVESTED IN A HOME FOR A DESERVING FAMILY

1985-2005

TWENTY YEARS OF BUILDING FUTURES IN OUR COMMUNITY ONE HOME AT A TIME

1200 SQUARE FOOT HOUSE @ $65,000 = $54.17 PER SQUARE FOOT
This certificate represents a tax deductible donation. It has no cash value.

YES, I WOULD LIKE TO HELP!

I support the work that Habitat for Humanity does and I want to be part of the excitement! As a donor, I will receive periodic updates on your construction activities but, more importantly, I know my gift will help a family in our community realize the dream of homeownership. **I would like to SHARE in your efforts against substandard housing in my community!** *(Please print below)*

PLEASE SEND ME _____ SHARES at $54.17 EACH = $ $_____

In Honor Of: _____

Occasion: (Circle One)   HOLIDAY   BIRTHDAY   ANNIVERSARY

     OTHER: _____

Address of Recipient: _____

Gift From: _____ *Donor Address:* _____

Donor Email: _____

I AM ENCLOSING A CHECK FOR $ $_____ PAYABLE TO HABITAT FOR HUMANITY **OR** PLEASE CHARGE MY VISA OR MASTERCARD *(CIRCLE ONE)*

Card Number _____ Expiration Date: _____

Name as it appears on Credit Card _____ Charge Amount $ _____

Signature _____

Billing Address _____

Telephone # Day _____ Eve _____

PLEASE NOTE: Your contribution is tax-deductible to the fullest extent allowed by law.
Habitat for Humanity • P.O. Box 1443 • Newport News, VA 23601 • 757-596-5553
www.HelpHabitatforHumanity.org